Published   in   2020   by   FeedA]

Compiled on behalf of Laura Stephenson by Mike Barnes

Cover design by Ben Barnes

Dedicated to
Mark Stephenson,
Heidi Jessie Stephenson,
Naomi Eva Stephenson
and
Sophie Eliza Stephenson.

This book is testimony to the life of Laura Constance Stephenson.

Her faith was immense. Her courage was enormous. Her words will live on forever and make us all think about life, whether you have a faith as strong as Laura's or just a belief to be the best we can in this world.

Prologue

On Thursday 19th April 2018 I got a telephone call from Laura as she was coming away from her appointment with the consultant. He gave her the news that she had Stage 4 Bowel cancer. When she called, Laura and her husband, Mark, were in the car on their way home to give the news to Mark's mum and dad and to Laura's mum. At the time I was in Malawi, volunteering on behalf of Voluntary Services Overseas. As you can imagine, the telephone call was not an easy one.

"I don't want this, Dad. I want to see my girls grow up. I want to see them get married." And when you're that distance away all you can say is,

"You will! I promise. You will!" Needless to say I caught the first flight home.

From that day onward, Laura fought with all her might and strength to do just that. As the days progressed, so did her faith in God that would help her throughout this journey. A God that would guide her in every footstep she took, every decision she took and every moment of her day.

Sister to Emily and Harriet – "inspirational and beautiful", wife of Mark, "superhero" and mother of Heidi "my very own angel", and twins, Sophie and Naomi, 'my two warriors', Laura was born to be a model 'Mum'. After being diagnosed with Bowel cancer she was determined to not let anything get in the way of looking after her three daughters. Many a time the offer to pick Heidi up from school, or offer to look after Naomi and Sophie for a short while was made. The answer was always the same. "No thanks I can do it. I'm fine."
Cancer was not going to stop her being 'a Mummy'.

She always engaged in friendly chats with other parents in the playground. Their response was always how cheerful she was, how positive she was and how strong her faith was. It made no difference who she was speaking to, different cultures, religions, race. The response from those she spoke to, was always the same; a person of huge faith, positivity and conviction. She became a true friend of many whom she met just briefly at the start and end of the school day.
Cancer was not going to stop her relationships with those around her.

3

Employed as a fund raiser for a local cancer charity, she often saw it as an opportunity to talk to others not only about the charity but about how to manage living with a diagnosis of cancer and the treatments which inevitably follow. She was determined to carry on working. She enjoyed talking to people, from large corporate bodies to individuals, all interested and keen to support the work of the charities as well as to get to know her personally.

Cancer was not going to stop her working.

Being diagnosed with Bowel cancer back in April 2018, she was told that the tumours were too advanced for surgery at that time and the only current course of action was to have fortnightly courses of Chemotherapy. She would spend many an hour talking to those others alongside her undergoing chemotherapy. She would often come away from these appointments absolutely bubbling, having shared discussions which either developed into her offering words of comfort and support to those she was talking to, or alternatively receiving their support.

Cancer was not going to stop her helping those around her.

From a very early age Laura had a very strong Christian faith. This faith just grew and grew with every day. It was always important but became vital to Laura in her 'fight' against this 'enemy' that had developed in her body. Whenever anyone said, "How can God let this happen to you?", she would always respond with "God is as angry about this as I am, and he is fighting alongside me and with me."

Cancer was not going to make her question her belief.

Following on from two brief stays in hospital, Laura came home on December 20th 2019. Christmas was spent with her family. On Christmas day, Heidi, Sophie and Naomi opened their presents with their Mum and Dad. Presents which had recently been purchased by Mum and Dad together, on behalf of Father Christmas. The girls played with their toys while "Mum and Dad' watched and joined in.

Cancer was not going to stop Christmas

On Saturday December 28th 2019 Laura's body lost its fight.

After being diagnosed in April, many friends and family said that Laura should be recording her actions and thoughts. She started to write her first blog in August 2018.

Warriordiaries.co.uk was started.

This book is a compilation of those blogs.

All quotes in this book are Laura's or collected from people who knew Laura.

My thanks to everyone who has contributed to this book; many unknowingly.

My thanks to my family for their support and help in those moments when I couldn't type due to the tears. It is in those moments that Laura took over and helped me compile it.

My thanks to Mark, Heidi, Sophie and Naomi for being the amazing people that they are.

Most of all my love and thanks to Laura, for being the most incredible human being that I have ever known.

Dad x

04/09/1983 - 28/12/2019

On December 28th I (Dad) promised Laura I would write the next post in her blog. I don't know if she heard me but I'm pretty sure she did. I actually said to her that I couldn't do as good a job as she did, and just the look on her face said it all .... "Of course you can Dad"

And that was Laura to a tee, giving people confidence, hope, to do whatever they thought they couldn't do. I guess similar to what I had done to her as she was growing up, encouragement to achieve, succeed at whatever you set your mind to do, and go for it.

However, I know that on this occasion she was wrong and I really wont write the words as well as she could - so my apologies Lol, but I did try!

Most of you who read this will know that on December 28th 2019 Laura's body could no longer sustain her life. I use those words carefully. Laura's diaries were called Warrior Diaries for a reason. She was in a battle; she knew she was. She wasn't a lone warrior, she had support from a huge army of family, friends and most of all the support of her faith, her belief in God, The Saviour, as they all battled against the cancer that was enveloping her body. It was through this faith that she won the battle. Her faith stayed with her until her body breathed its last breath and she entered into the Kingdom of the Lord

7

Laura's positivity for life was inspiring. It rubbed off on all she met. I don't think in the twenty months of her battle did I ever hear a negative comment about her illness.

Never an excuse; never an "...if only..." comment; never a "why me?" Yes, she would get cross but as in "I'm going to fight this" attitude. Yes, she had times when she questioned things but without doubt something would come along that would re-ignite that spark of hope, be it small or a blinding light, every time she felt unsure of her path the spark was there. She was constantly willing to share this light with everyone.

Her blogs absolutely portrayed her life; positivity, hope, faith, caring, thinking of others. All of them are a true testament to her life.

"How are you?" is the generic greeting usually given and Laura's response literally up to the last day of her life was "I'm fine. How are you?" I know she made me think hard about her words, as she did everyone she met. She lived her life as a shining example of her faith. Every discussion, with her, every deed she undertook, made those around her feel more positive.

Standing joke with Laura was that I would always "go round the houses" before getting to the punch line; so although I could, if pushed, not only go round the houses but along several streets as well, as a supremely "proud Dad" and with watering eyes I can safely say ....

Laura won the battle"

and this is her story ....

Warrior Diary

Since all this started people keep saying I need to write things down. My story. I'm not sure much of what I have to say will be interesting to all but I do know that I am seeing little God instances all the time. So before I start with those let me also say that I will unashamedly be talking about my walk with God throughout this journey because without Him it would be a battle without hope and I can tell you now that would be one scary path!　I, however, don't have to experience that because like my own Dad, I have a father in heaven, that would move mountains to heal me. With God **nothing** is **impossible**!

In the beginning He wanted to teach me about sitting in the boat with the waves crashing around me…. I remember sitting at traffic lights and Him shouting at me to stop sitting and to get out of the boat. I have read the story in Matthew and always understood that to walk on the water would require a huge amount of **faith**. That is what he was calling me to do, and the first lesson in all of this has been about expanding my faith. So that is what I have tried to do and by resting in His word (reading my bible) I have finally taken the step and leg lift needed to get out of **my** boat and am walking in **complete** faith on water!

My first story of seeing God move in this situation has to be my two fabulous friends I made in September at a baby group when unbeknownst to me I would be meeting them in a very different environment. These two lovely ladies do an amazing job as chemo nurses for me when I am in for treatment. They were placed in that baby group so that God knew I would have friendly faces looking after me in 8 months time when I needed it! **His** provision is amazing and so much better than my forward planning! #seeingGodgobeforeus #livinginfaith

August 11th 2018   Perfect position ….

I am placed in the PERFECT position now to help others. He knows what is needed for me to bless others while fighting this battle, so that's what I will do!　Last week was a big deal for me as I got my wig, my hair isn't gone but has thinned dramatically. After being told mixed messages over whether I would lose my hair or not I wasn't quite sure how I felt about it.

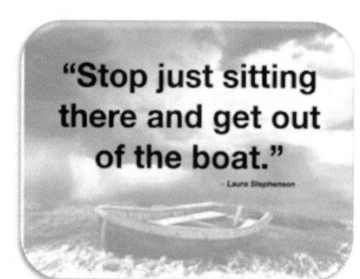

"Stop just sitting there and get out of the boat."
– Laura Stephenson

"What an amazing person. A demonstration of trust, love and hope. Laura has touched my own life so much. Her incredible faith and positivity were courageous."

I had two mini tears moments with Mark but other than that, figure it looks ok and it isn't forever so let's get cracking!

After purchasing the chosen locks, I was in work the next day when I got a phone call from an upset daughter of a lady who had been diagnosed with breast cancer. Mother and daughter were panicking about losing hair and wearing a wig. It was great to say "I did that yesterday, it's not too bad". All of these are my opinions but I do believe that in this position. GOD has great plans for people for me to bless and engage in conversations that have impact and support! Not a path I would have ever chosen but man am I excited to see what He has in store not only for those I come into contact with but ultimately for my complete HEALING!

August 12th 2018 –   Trust in Him

This is just what I needed today, after a bit of a tearful blip last night, think tiredness had taken over, I need to remember he has this and I can wholeheartedly **trust** in **his promises**! He has never failed me yet! Just look at the three beautiful girls I have! How could I doubt **him**! Beautiful friends have reminded me today; I don't have to have this all figured out or be positive every second of the day. He holds me close enough that I can hear his heartbeat! Amazing!

August 17th 2018   David and Goliath

 There aren't many times I let these side effects get to me but last night I can honestly say I was exhausted so at 8pm bedtime beckoned and I took it! I must admit I don't have a massive problem with chemo. It's a necessity and it's making this thing go, so I figure may as well just get on with it. I also get a good three hours a week of quiet reading time so who can complain at that with three children who keep you on the go! I think what makes my chemo sessions even more interesting is the people I am meeting. The last few times I have met someone just embarking on this journey and looking terrified. I'm not sure I was as terrified but I think the fear of not knowing what you will feel like at the end of the cycle often adds to this fear. I have loved chatting to people and hopefully helping to put their mind at ease. There really is nothing to fear of chemo, you manage the side effects and aim to not let them take on a mind of their own by bringing you down in your spirit. I don't really think too much of what these horrible chemicals are doing to my body as they may be nasty but they need to be to destroy that bigger mountain of tumours.

It's a little like David and Goliath! We all know how that story ended! When you think of it like that and consider all the words in the bible, 'faith as small as a mustard seed can move a mountain' it doesn't matter how little that chemo may be because it's often the little things that make the biggest impact!

My faith is huge. With that and a little chemo (for as long as it's needed) I know that this thing is totally beatable! In fact, it doesn't stand a chance against the **power** and **might** of my God!

August 18th 2018   Run with ….

Therefore, since we are surrounded by such a great cloud of witnesses, let us throw off everything that hinders and the sin that so easily entangles. And let us run with perseverance the race marked out for us - Hebrews 12:1

This verse has been spoken over me in the past for pushing forward and running... but never have I heard it spoken like this. Sometimes when things get spoken over us or we are given a word we push it to one side as if God didn't really want us to hear it or maybe He gave it to lots of people and not for my situation. I accept this as a word from God that he wants me to continue to push into **his word**, and I will not give up. I will not do this journey complaining, I will strive to listen to Him and trust that he will bring me out the other side complete in His healing power! He has a plan for me and it is to bring him glory!

As you can tell I love this blessing this evening and it has given me a real boost that his work in me is not done yet! How exciting!!

"Laura was a truly wonderful young lady. It was an honour to have known her. She is and will remain a really positive influence in many, many lives"

Beautiful friends have reminded me today, I don't have to have this all figured out or be positive every second of the day

–Laura Stephenson

August 21st 2018   Making an impact

Love that everything I do, say and act makes an impact! People say I am really positive but that's only because like this post says, **my** faith matters to God so why would I be anything but positive when He sees it all and will always keep his promises to me if I allow my faith to be big enough

August 25th 2018   In Awe

When I started this journey there was so much to take in and different things that may help. It's been so interesting to explore new things but ultimately to start thinking about my body and the amazing creation that it is. **He** made me so fearfully and wonderfully!

My body is taking a huge beating in all of this, from dry skin, cracking finger tips, a sore face and multiple mouth ulcers! Sometimes it is drained but most of the time it just keeps going on fighting off this imposter in my body.

And I am so in awe of his creation!

When you are fighting something like this it is important to take care of what God created. So I am doing all I can. I have turmeric tablets that aid in a healthy body. Bitter apricot kernels, are great at fighting this thing off. They taste disgusting and they do have some bits that aren't great but taken in small quantities they are ok. The honey to aid my immune system (was on 'This Morning', and I love that doctor on there) It seems to be working as I haven't missed a chemo session yet! Countless smoothies full of fruit, spinach and good stuff, some taste good others not so much. Then there are the broccoli seeds that have the best bits of the alkaline stuff to provide an environment that cancer can't grow in. And the trampette helps me to clear those pesky lymph nodes that need to sort themselves out. My next step is alkaline water - if I make an environment in there that it can't survive in. It's giving my body the best opportunity to kill what shouldn't be there. All in all, my body is amazing, even with the bits that shouldn't now be in there and for that I have my God to thank! HE created me perfectly

14

and HE will finish the great works that he has started in me! All of the above helps but **prayer** and total **faith** in him will see me come out the other side.

August 28th 2018   In a storm

Today I really feel that I am meant to be learning about praise. Praising God in hard times can be difficult. It's not easy when you are in a storm with waves raging around you and you feel like you want to see an outcome immediately. But my God doesn't always work like that, sometimes He does things in His own timing. That isn't always easy to stomach but it isn't ours to question either. Why would I question the God who created me perfectly and sees the bigger picture? I don't know the people He might get me to meet or talk too in the time that I am going through this and just maybe there is someone down the road that may really need a small word of support.

So in all of this, raising praise to our God is a different way to approach this, but today He has definitely taught me to sing out my praise to Him. It lifts Him up and gives Him the glory! I get excited to be able to praise Him. He is in all of this and I love being able to sing it out... It makes me happy and my spirit gets a real boost to sing words that are loaded with so much power.

"This is how I fight my battles! It may look like I'm surrounded but I'm surrounded by you." Surrounded – Michael W. Smith

August 28th 2018   A LITTLE WOBBLE

Every time I have a wobble or feel a little unsettled I am reminded of this!
Today I saw a consultant who wasn't sure I should have been prescribed the face cream that I am currently on. As you all know the tablets I have been having didn't do much and this new cream means my girls can kiss or touch my face without me being in pain. It isn't sore when I do yoga, and it doesn't hurt when I smile. If I had had this same consultant two weeks ago I may not have had the cream I had. Now consultants are just being cautious and I understand and thank them for that

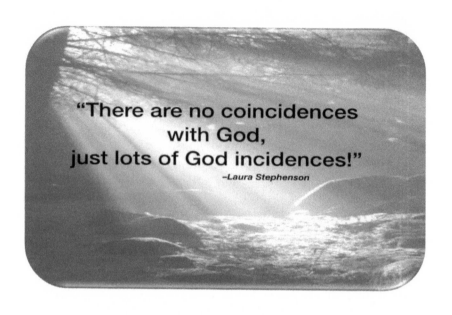

"There are no coincidences
with God,
just lots of God incidences!"
–Laura Stephenson

"I have been awestruck by her positivity, faith and hope -- I'm not sure I will ever witness anything like it again"

"We feel Laura has been an inspiration to us and has touched our lives forever. A very special person who will never be forgotten."

...However I believe God saw my pain and gave me a consultant who wanted to try something and I praise the Lord that he did! There are no coincidences with God just lots of God incidences! Woo hoo sorry lots of posts tonight! #sorrynotsorry

September 3rd 2018   Nothing to fear

My Pump
So this is my pump … (it's a balloon in a plastic tube ! Love my stylish bag for it though!) I realised the other day that some may not know what the treatment I am currently having looks like or contains! To be fair I had no idea, even working in cancer charities as I have for the last 5 years what chemotherapy involved! I am currently on three drugs in each cycle, an immunotherapy drug, 5FU (Fulfury) and irinotecan. The Fulfury one is a drug that needs to be administered over a period of 46 hours following the two hours I have at the cancer centre. It needs to be done like this as it can do more harm if given too quickly.

Now I could moan about the side effects of these drugs (which aren't many for me at the moment). However, they are helping, with a lot of prayer, to fight this thing and to get rid of it for me!! Therefore, I'm not dwelling on that. I need it and it's doing its job. When the nurses ask me how I am finding them I simply say I love the four hours of reading I get once a week in peace and quiet!

Someone in the chemo unit was having a little moan last week about how annoying the pump can be to have attached to you for 46 hours, but to me it doesn't stop me from doing anything. (ok things can be trickier!) It is a necessity and I am so blessed to be able to get this treatment on the National Health Service and in complete comfort! It's become my little sidekick in this fight and man am I fighting !

17

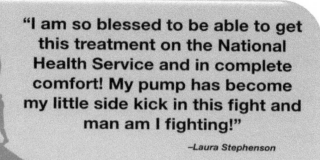

"I am so blessed to be able to get this treatment on the National Health Service and in complete comfort! My pump has become my little side kick in this fight and man am I fighting!"

–Laura Stephenson

"You were a true inspiration to all the District Nurses. It was a pleasure to care for you. We will share your strength and words with others"

"Your strength, belief and hope will be carried and spoken about to our patients. You are truly inspirational and your inspiration will live on; we will carry your word."

Now don't get me wrong sometimes it's ok to have a little moan or feel a bit discouraged. Sometimes I get bogged down in thoughts of, 'I have no idea what these drugs are doing to me long term or if they will continue to be as effective as they are currently being.'
However, one thing I am confident of: is that I know that I have **nothing** to fear.

Nothing to fear and a fighting attitude. Now imagine what could be accomplished if we took up that sword of **confident faith**, put down our 'woe is me' attitude and kicked some butt! We would be limitless in our adventure through this life. Nothing would slow us down. If only we could se that bigger glorious picture that is planned for us.

Have a good weekend everyone.!

September 9th 2018   Positivity

People keep telling me that I am so positive about things and I am never quite sure how to respond…. I can say that I don't feel like that every day and some days I have to work hard at it. The thing is with being positive; it is a choice. We have the freedom to choose how we approach something. Now don't get me wrong I have days just like everyone else where our stresses and problems seem like this huge weight on your shoulders and we just can't shift it, and so it affects our mood too..

But being given the freedom to choose how we face those things in front of us, is something that I wouldn't swop for anything. It allows me to FIGHT and to make sure that each day, regardless of how I feel, I am standing steadfast in the promises that are given to me. How amazing that I get to choose how I want to deal with something! And every time I choose **faith** over fear, **hope** over worry and **belief** over doubt.

It's not always easy but it is definitely worth it. Plus, through **grace** it's a free gift!

"People keep telling me that I am so positive about things and I am never quite sure how to respond..... I can say that I don't feel like that every day and some days I have to work hard at it. "

– Laura Stephenson

"The thing is with being positive; it is a choice. We have the freedom to choose how we approach something ...

being given the freedom to choose how we face those things in front of us, is something that I wouldn't swop for anything ....

every time I choose faith over fear, hope over worry and belief over doubt."

– Laura Stephenson

"Through her faith she never seemed to grumble or moan. May her life of positivity stay in each of her family and friends lives."

"A true inspiration. The girls will be so proud when they are old enough to hear about their amazing mum."

"I followed your journey and was truly inspired by your bravery and strength. You will always have a special place in my heart."

"You have been an absolute rock to us all, especially me. I say to your girls, 'Your mother was one of the most special people I've ever met!'.

September 12th 2018   Bouncing

So following chemo I have two ways to shock those lymph nodes into action; my trampette and the power of **my** God. I know He will put in His side of this so I should probably get bouncing to keep up mine 😌 😂 #smashingthis #lymphnodesgetinline
Turns out there is something about bouncing that opens up your lymph nodes so therefore in faith that He is working in me I thought why sit

around I may as well bounce! I have had a tough few days for various reasons but God has continued to speak to me. I have had two very close friends give me some wonderful words unaware of the rubbish thoughts I've had. Does it ever seem like we are listening to the wrong things or putting our trust in the worldly things?! Then God steps in and brings me just what I need without a second thought. He uses people in my world to speak to me, to give me a word that helps lift me up and brings my faith to a whole new level.

September 14th 2018   Cause and effect

Someone asked me this week 'what do you think it is, that's having such an impact on your results?' In that moment I stood not sure what to say, now don't get me wrong I **know** that anything shrinking or in the case of my lung tumour disappearing is all down to the **power** of my God. He has never left my side, failed me or abandoned me and He wouldn't start now. However, I do also believe that there is a place for health remedies and the fabulous NHS. God has placed doctors, nurses and fabulous people in my path to help me through this with their knowledge and wisdom. They know their medical facts. (Not the truth but a lot of good stuff!)

I replied good food, research, health remedies, chemotherapy and a lot of PRAYER. This leads me to where I am today with my thoughts. I went to a prayer meeting last night and really felt the power of God in that room. I don't often do gushing God posts but this is one.

I have been blown away by the amount of people praying for me at the moment, from New Zealand, Africa, Spain and France to right here on my door step of the UK! How incredible that we can stand together in everything that we face in this life with others all round the world! What a blessing and privilege to share life with people who want to see Gods miracles ripple across this world never mind their home cities!

I am so amazed that their prayer continues; that they offer up their words to God to see my miracle come to fruition! Thank you from the bottom of my heart. It is such a boost and you are amazing for adding me into your prayers!

My verse for today

"We all experience times of testing, which is normal for every human being. But God will be faithful to you. He will screen and filter the severity, nature, and timing **of** every test or trial you face so that you can bear it. And each test is an opportunity to trust him more, for along with every trial God has provided for you a way **of** escape that will bring you out **of** it victoriously."

Corinthians 1 – 10-13
        Prayers are powerful because they are filled with truth from the word. They allow us to have a constant relationship with our Heavenly Father who just wants he best for his children. He is a good God, nothing bad including sickness can come from him because He is only good.

Moving forward I think when someone asks me that question again my reply needs to start with FAITH, pure and simple my FAITH and that of others. It's what is making this huge difference to my walk through cancer to the other side.

"How incredible that we can stand together in everything that we face in this life with others all round the world! What a blessing and privilege to share life with people who want to see Gods miracles ripple across this world never mind their home cities!."
– Laura Stephenson

"She made me bold and courageous just being around her. Awesome woman and mother."
"You impacted our lives so much with your faith, strength and even support while you had a huge mountain to climb of your own; it was inspirational!"

So there are two posts I have in my head to write that I think God has placed on my heart this week through things I have listened to. Please excuse any spelling issues as the skin on my thumb has cracked and it's hard to type! (That's my excuse and I'm sticking to it)

My first post this evening is that through all of this I am being taught about relationships. Now my whole job is about relationships so I wasn't sure how much more there could be to learn but once again when I think I know best I get a gentle nudge to say 'have you thought about it from this angle' and my mind gets blown to a new way of seeing something! I love being social, chatting and catching up with friends. God knows this and uses it totally for his glory!

He has placed in my path recently some quite amazing friends, family that are constantly there for me all times of the day or night and through work there are people I would never have encountered encouraging me positively forward. I can ask all of these people questions, they challenge me, encourage me and are on this track of healing with me.

When you start off on this path, many people find it hard to understand or comprehend that I am not falling apart, fearful or scared. The idea of healing is so foreign to us that some people don't know how to handle my response 'I have a God that **will** heal me', so they look at me with sad eyes and ask 'How are you really doing?' I find this really tough to handle as it makes me feel fearful and uneasy. And It's not that they don't care about my feelings or are even aware they are making me upset by asking. In fact, I think it's their way of showing me love and I love them for that.

The relationships that I have at the moment in this with me, whether they have a faith or aren't quite there yet, are what keeps me going. They are extraordinary and I know God uses every single one just when I need it most!

Thank you from the bottom of my heart to all of you that are praying for me, encouraging me, making me laugh, inspiring me, letting me rant, serving me and being the amazing group of people doing life with me!

25

God is using you in the most wonderful way so I thank you for letting him and loving others in such a way that it makes you shine

September 18th 2018 …… BUT WHO YOU KNOW

My second post is a thank you to my amazing family & close friends. I am always in awe of you all. How selfless, generous and kind you all are is what keeps the five of us going. Never underestimate how incredible you all are, take time to know that you are real blessings to us and we would be lost without you.

It would be remiss of me to not mention and save space in this post to also gush about my partner in crime in this journey. My husband has to be one of the best out there! I honestly believe I have married superman! He is definitely my superhero! It must be pretty scary for him as much as it could be for me in this... and yet I am blessed to have married a man who is on the same page in my healing. This is no small thing! He gets what I need. He always loves me (even when I don't get up in the middle of the night with the twins!) and he says all the right things just when I need them most! He is such a strength to all four of us, he doesn't complain or tire of being that rooted person for us as a family. I am so blessed by him, and when I am having an off moment he just sits and lets me have that time without feeling like he needs to fix it for me. Thank you for being this wonderful blessing to the four of us and for being the best person for me on this journey! Let's smash this in His glory!

Thank you from the bottom of my heart to all of you that are praying for me, encouraging me, making me laugh, inspiring me, letting me rant, serving me and being the amazing group of people doing life with me!

– *Laura Stephenson*

"I feel like we shared a journey. You have encouraged me to be better, more positive and more forgiving. Thank You."

"She was sat on a bean-bag, a little tipsy, laughing and being silly. I hadn't known her for long but loved that she felt chilled enough to be able rock-up, enjoy herself and be silly. I count it as a privilege to have been with her."

September 22nd 2018   FEAR HAS NO PLACE

Today I went, with Heidi, to 'Clip and climb". It got me thinking about my walk in all of this. My eldest daughter as many of you might know isn't the most daring of children, to be fair she is a little bit of a wimp with new things and quite cautious in her approach to most things. We arrived and she immediately clung to my clothes. She kept saying, "Mummy I don't want to do this"; "Mummy stay with me". Now again as most of you will know my response was not going to be one of, "You don't have to do this". No, I crouched down looked her in the eyes and said, "Stop being silly, give it a go and you will be fine!"

It may sound like I didn't care that she was fearful or unsure, which is of course not the case at all. But I know that sometimes Heidi needs that extra push to try something. My love for Heidi is unconditional, and exceeds anything that I ever imagined, but in that moment she needed a Mummy that would push her to try something, face that little bit of fear she had and step forward.

For me, I am fearful occasionally. I don't quite know how to approach this mountain in front of me and I need a gentle push from the boat to get out onto the water. That push comes from my Heavenly Father. He **loves** me unconditionally and knows what is best for me. He knows that my fear is not built on truth, it comes from uncertainty and it has no strength against **faith**. I need to trust him just like Heidi trusts me, He will not let me fall!

The second thing he taught me today was about fear. When Heidi looked at that wall in front of her she was fearful because she didn't trust the safety harness to hold her. She also climbed and then wasn't quite sure how to get down. The cable attached to her would help her if she just leant back and let go.

But how scary is that to do sometimes? Just lean back and let go of the one thing that is keeping you on a firm footing! Yet in that moment I realised that often my fears rise because I am trusting a mountain to hold me up and not God. I need to trust that my safety harness which is **Him** is securely fastened and I cannot fall!

28

And the cable that attaches you to the wall, so that when you get to the top you can just push off with your feet, let go with your hands and drop slowly back down to the ground; Heidi was secure in the knowledge that this would not let her fall in a heap and was her safety!

We have our very own cable and we are attached to the almighty presence of the Lord, by **His** word and **His** Promises. We cannot fall because we have the best secure line directly to Him. What have we to fear when we are connected to Him - they are **His** promises and **His love** never fails!

So often I let fear creep in through thoughts of what happens if my lymph nodes don't respond or if my liver just pushes this thing further into my body. But that fear has **no** place in my thoughts and it will not push out any of the **faith** that I have because I am connected to the most **steadfast** safety line. When I can **trust** that He has this covered, good things come from him and His truth is written out plainly for me to see - By His stripes I am **healed**!

At the end of the session, my daughter turned round to me with the biggest smile on her face and said, "Can we come again tomorrow Mummy?"
Such joy in knowing that fear has no place when you can confidently trust that you will come to no harm when you are resting in the presence of God.

October 1st 2018   STAND BY ME

Today was a mixed day of emotion, I had a consultant appointment to talk about things. I think sometimes we get a bit used to hearing the same things or complacent in our walk with the Lord. It's not a bad thing, but sometimes it makes us lose sight of what we are doing or the battle we are fighting. Today I was reminded that I am in a storm, that this is a battle and that to come out the other side I must press into **His** presence and word more than ever!

Without dwelling too much on what was said or the way it made me feel, I will just give you all an update. Basically my cancer blood marker, which shows if it is about to spread further or there will be changes to what it is doing (i.e. not continuing to shrink or responding), is increasing. There are other factors that could be nothing, that would make this increase but it is also one for the doctors to be concerned about if you have cancer.

It really gave me a sucker punch feeling in my stomach and left me feeling uncertain. But even in the midst of that I kept up the mantra in my head, '**Healing** is mine'.

Then as always **God** steps in and reminds me that **He** has the power in this and I don't need to have that feeling in my stomach. I got back to work from the meeting, feeling rubbish and a lady came into our office. Our door isn't often left open but she asked after a colleague. The colleague had gone out, so I offered my help, told her who I was and she told me who she was. She looked me in the eye, and said, "Oh **you** are Laura"! She then proceeded to tell me that, "It is all in His hands and it is all in His timing". I have never met this lady before and I certainly didn't ask for her thoughts on my faith but God knew in that moment that I need affirmation and He delivered.

I really felt today that God wants me to remember, my healing, will happen in His timing. He gave me a picture today, that someone gave to me a while ago but was raised in my mind this afternoon. When you fly, before you rise above the clouds, the weather around you can be bleak, dull & stormy. But once above those clouds the sun can be bright, illuminating and shining. I am in a storm that looks bleak to those around me, it's turbulent and sometimes it's tough to be there. However even though I haven't seen my sun rise on this miracle yet: **It will**. The time is coming when I will see the glorious light of the sun shining on this storm and it will be total healing because that is what **He** promises!

I have heard your prayers and seen your tears; I will *heal* you

2 Kings 20:7

30

"But once above those clouds the sun can be bright, illuminating and shining.

I haven't seen my sun risen on this miracle yet: It will.

The time is coming when I will see the glorious light of the sun shining on this storm."

– Laura Stephenson

Thank you for standing with me and for continued prayers. It means so much to me! You are all amazing!

"When you fly, before you rise above the clouds, the weather around you can be bleak, dull & stormy."

– Laura Stephenson

This week has been a tough one, and not because I have felt particularly down but I think because I let fear in and man is it hard to push it out once you let it in!

But I listened to a very wise lady who said, "It's ok to feel fear, in fact it is totally natural in a situation where you are surrounded to feel that way. What you don't want to do is sit down and make friends with it or let it hang around too long!" This has been true of this week, whilst I may feel fear **I will not** allow it to steal my joy or my positivity or worst of all any of my **faith**!

I have listened to songs and podcasts, had some amazing support from friends and then reading this tonight got me thinking even more. I knew this whole journey would be a roller coaster. There will be ups and downs but one thing I know for certain is I will fight. And what if my fighting spirit is scaring the enemy? What if when I go out and say, "Yes it is looking worse but you know I have a God that HEALS" or to those doctors that want to give me the harsh facts I say, 'Thanks but I'm not afraid because HE created me perfectly'.

I have come to the realisation this week that my approach in all of this terrifies the enemy because I might just sow a seed in someone's mind that **God** gave his son for **you**! They might see someone approaching what should be terrifying, differently and wonder why or how that is possible...

To think I might just show more than a few people the light that is my God is amazing but equally that kind of power and influence is not quite what the enemy had in mind and he wants to stop it in its tracks. So I say to you; "Cancer **I will not** stop fighting you. Enemy **I will not** stop praising God. Fear, you can keep walking because you are not welcome to stop and rest at my door!"

I will see healing and miracles, because my God is a God that keeps his promises!

So today I got some results back and they show that at least three of my tumours have shrunk with the one on the lung almost completely gone! These are some God glory amazing results! However, I am focussed on the fact that my lymph nodes have yet to get the memo on the what they should be doing and that there is a slight progression with them. Why when God wants us to see his splendour and the work he is doing in us, are we focused on disappointment? I am not under any illusion that I am currently listening to the wrong whispers in my ear! I need to tell those whispers to do one, and focus on the one simple truth

"I pray with great faith for you, because I'm fully convinced that the One who began this glorious work in you will **faithfully** continue the process of maturing you and will put his finishing touches to it until the unveiling of our Lord Jesus Christ!" Philippians 1: 6

He, who started this work in me, will see it to completion. **I trust His word**! I have faith in it and I need to start listening to the whispers that build me up, give me strength and push me forward in my faith. These results are amazing, and I give him the glory, fully trusting that this is stepping further out on the water of faith and it will all go!

October 12th 2020 The Power of ....

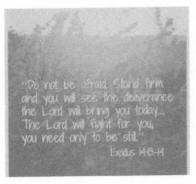

Had an amazing night of prayer last night. I am surrounded by such a great team of women and they are such a blessing.

I will post a longer message later but I have been taught this week about the importance of getting up to pray in the morning and asking for blessings every morning.

"It's ok to feel fear, in fact it is totally natural in a situation where you are surrounded to feel that way. What you don't want to do is sit down and make friends with it or let it hang around too long!"."
–Laura Stephenson

"There were times when I came to visit, that Laura would be at home feeling poorly from chemo but I was always greeted with, 'Hi Lovely'. No matter what she was going through she always made me feel positive and inspired. Laura has taught me how to live life to the full".

So here it is for the morning, may it bless you as it has blessed me! Big day with God today, but I feel the winds of change He is blowing across this path, there will be healing today and it will be unexplained except for His glory shining through!

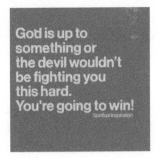

God is up to something or the devil wouldn't be fighting you this hard. You're going to win!
Spiritual Inspiration

October 17ᵗʰ 2018   HOW DO YOU KNOW

This post has been a long time in coming and I haven't really known how to write it! Not because it's bad or negative, in fact far from it. But God has been teaching me things that I need to get in some kind of order (still doesn't make much sense) so that I could explain where the path is taking me next...

Through all of this, reading my bible has become so much more than it ever used to be. I was, I hate to admit, one of those who would pick up my bible every now and four months time and was never sure what I was meant to read. And it never really spoke to me. I read it and then would ask God to use it but I never felt the connection. It has become my go to now in this battle. I love reading books that support the word but more than ever I love finding those verses that jump out of the page at me! It's those verses that are **his promises**. How incredible that it is filled with **promises**! And our God is a God that doesn't break promises!

Whenever I have heard preachers on reading your bible and it being part of the armour of God, I listened but never took it in. How can we put on an armour, and what does that mean?

Well simply put I believe that when we face battle, which is most days, let's **stand** in those promises in **His** word! Why would we not? By standing on His word, it means we **learn** verses. We read odd verses maybe from something we see on Pinterest or something we remember from a song at church. Google it, find out where in the bible that verse is and learn it. **God** is trying to teach us every day with His word but we just get too busy to stop and read! So I have started to stick post-its up in our house!

The next bit of my post is all about a church service I went to in Walsall at the weekend. Andrew Womack was preaching, not on healing but he is a big advocate that we already have the power and authority to be healed. So after my manic Saturday night organising our charity ball I decided that regardless of sleep needed I had to be there! We got there early, which wasn't planned, and sat around having a brew before we went into the hall. After a while we decided to go and get a seat. There had been phone calls prior to the date from Mark's uncle about me having prayer from Andrew but it wasn't guaranteed and they said he may not be able to, as the venue would be packed with over 1,000 people. As we walked in, Andrew Womack was stood in the doorway praying for someone so we saw this and took it! I waited to speak to him, told him what was wrong in my body. He asked if I had any pain, to which I said no not at all. And he then asked,

'So how do you know you have cancer?'

That question will stick with me forever! In the midst of all of this I am trusting the word of humans. Now don't get me wrong, I know the scans show what is in my body, but if I **know** I will be healed why am I trusting them with their results and not having belief in what is written in the word!

He prayed for me to be healed quickly, and he prayed for the damage that has been done to my other organs through the treatment. This is something I have worried about for ages, but not voiced to Andrew. So to have a prayer over that was amazing! He was prompted by **my** God!

The service was about getting our minds to be in line with the word so that our bodies can match up! If we stand in the word of God, then our bodies will start to respond to that and fall in line. How we shouldn't beg for something when it is already given. If I give you my bible, and then you look at me with my bible in your hand and ask for my bible. I would probably look at you a bit confused! So God is no different! He says we are healed so why would we keep asking! He talked about Authority, the Holy Spirit and the power of Jesus Christ in us! We have the authority to HEAL ourselves because we have been filled by the Holy Spirit and we have the power of Jesus within us!

"But forget all that— it is nothing compared to what I am going to do.
For I am about to do something new.
See, I have already begun! Do you not see it?
I will make a pathway through the wilderness.
I will create rivers in the dry wasteland."

Philippians 43: 18

It was amazing to hear things that God wanted to say to me, everything for that day lined up so I got to hear from God. Little miracles like Amy not having to take Ashton (her son) to football that day, Mark's Uncle saying he would drive and wanting to go even when I hadn't told him I was going, and being there an hour early to be greeted by Andrew.

"For I know the plans I have for you," declares the LORD, plans to prosper you and not to harm you, plans to give you hope and a future." Jeremiah 29:11

I was meant to be there and to hear all that was said! With the length of this post you can probably see why it has taken me so long to write! Sorry it's been a real week of revelation and I am so excited of what is to come!

October 24th 2018   FEAR AND FEELINGS

This morning I have been worshipping and listening to a podcast by a wonderful lady. In so many instances we face each day with fear, it is an overwhelming feeling that can often encourage us to drown under the weight of that feeling. But what if we acknowledged the feeling, feel it for a moment and then tell it to go. Sounds simple but it is anything but simple and it isn't easy. However, it doesn't mean we have to sit with that feeling.

"In all of these things we are more than CONQUERERS, through HIM that loved us"

Romans 8: 37

We can win the battle that fear is telling us we can't! Because maybe it is a feeling that once felt we should be commanding to leave us!

God wants to give us gifts, and he would never give us a gift of fear. So if he hasn't given us it, and yet there is a situation that continually makes us fearful, then it is trying to prevent us from going to the other side of that situation. The enemy is trying to prevent us from reaching the promises God has for us. So whenever I feel that fear, I find a promise in the word and use it as a shield to prevent it from affecting the rest of my day. It isn't easy but it is totally worth it, to sit in the word of God

"In so many instances we face each day with fear, it is an overwhelming feeling that can often encourage us to drown under the weight of that feeling. But what if we acknowledged the feeling, feel it for a moment and then tell it to go. "

– *Laura Stephenson*

"On a very very long charity walk, she met us and walked the last few miles. What a strong and courageous girl she is. A memory that will last with me."

"Sounds simple, but it is anything but simple, and it isn't easy. However it doesn't mean we have to sit with that feeling."

–*Laura Stephenson*

I haven't written for a while and I realised that might look to people like I'm struggling or not sure what to write because it's negative. That isn't the case at all, I have been moved and touched by God so much recently. He is doing some great works! I had results on Monday which were positive, my lymph nodes have started to respond praise God! Also my liver is shrinking and the bowel is stable. My blood cancer marker levels have increased but even the consultant said I didn't think we would have positive news to give you. You don't know **my God**. He is working in my body and He will not finish until those works are complete!

So yesterday while watching Heidi at gymnastics I was reading a book about Miracles in wastelands. God prompted me to check in on a friend by sending her a message about eagles and soaring high. In response it turned out the day before God had given her a picture to save to her phone; you guessed it. It was an eagle! As I continued to read God prompted me to understand that in this time, while I know the end result of healing is already given, I am in a wasteland that looks bleak but that **He** is stretching me, growing my faith and understanding of Him, all the time which is so exciting.

The post attached is the passage from the book I am reading, what a wonderful thing to be challenged by. I am not planted in this wasteland but I have a God that will carry me over bits of it when I need him too. At one point this week I needed that to happen.

I attended a conference for patients who are part of support groups in Lancashire, I used to organise this event when I worked at Rosemere Cancer Trust and even now I still am involved through my job as fundraiser. But essentially I attended as a patient this year. It was a fantastic conference with lots of information on research and not being afraid to ask about trials. I made some lovely contacts with people and had a good day. Up until the last consultant came to speak. She was ok. But half way through it became apparent she does what lots of consultants do and struggles to understand who her audience is. I think the words that hit me and many others were "chemotherapy doesn't cure cancer".

Now I'm not looking to chemo to cure me, because I have a higher power that has healed me. But it was a classic case of think before you speak who you are speaking too. There were ladies there still going through chemo and this really affected their spirits. I know what I believe but it can be hard to stand firm on that word when a wind blows against you. However, my trusty team of wonderful women rallied round me and sent messages to boost me. Making sure I was standing firm once again. I am blessed in all of this beyond measure by fabulous people, who message me, send cards and ring me to keep me standing on the word. I appreciate you all so much and you are huge blessings!

Chemo this week, let's see who He plans for me to meet!

Different schedule but one that is blessed with connections.

November 13th 2018   WAITING ON HIS WORD

Been learning lots this week, so watch this space for when it finally sinks in and I can write about it all...   Today I had an hour where I wasn't working, wasn't on a school run or providing cuddles for one of my girls. So I did what I find hardest to do and rested! I am not a resting type of girl, I like to be on the go and nipping somewhere or doing something to fill my time. But it got me thinking, why do we try to fill our lives with 'jobs' or tasks?! The rush of life has become all too familiar and sometimes all we need to do is slow down.

"Why do we try to fill our lives with 'jobs' or tasks? The rush of life has become all too familiar and sometimes all we need to do is slow down."

– Laura Stephenson

"She was always positive. If I doubted anything you could be sure Laura would change my mind and reassure me. How she did it I'll never know. She is an amazing mum to her three girls. A real super mum."

"I was in awe of Laura's upbeat, positive, determined, passionate outlook. Her love of life was evident. She exuded living with cancer. I left feeling uplifted by her."

Now I'm not saying that you should stop doing those things that make you feel useful or like you are achieving something. Many of us need that tick list to cross off those tasks we have done, and it can be the best feeling to know you have a day where you have achieved something! But what if we are missing out by not taking the time to rest?
Rest is not laziness, it is not being a coach potato or to do with being tired. Sometimes it is simply allowing ourselves to reflect. To just sit.

For me that is often a scary prospect but I am being taught that when I just sit, it is then that I can be taught. I learn more about the God that I serve in those times than I do at any other time in my life. In those times He speaks to me in a way that makes me sit up and listen. He is teaching me that rather than rushing into things, in order to receive from him we have to be willing to spend the time to just sit. We all have time to just sit.

We can't expect to receive from God if we don't spend the time being patient before Him. If we don't spend the time to meet with Him in this way imagine the blessings we are missing simply because we thought our 'jobs' were more important than what He has to give us! Being patient and just sitting is tough if you are an 'on the go' person but the rewards could be miraculous.

November 15th 2018

THERE ARE PEOPLE AND THEN THERE ARE PEOPLE

So today has been 'interesting' and it's only lunchtime! I met a lady. When I say met I was in a shop buying something and she was the lady on the till. She knew my family but I don't 'know' her in anyway really. Well what can I say about our conversation, stunned to silence I think probably covers it and she came across as 'a little nutty'. Now please don't think I am one for going about and banding that word around lightly. But when faced with someone who is going through treatment for cancer, you do not say "oh well chemotherapy doesn't work it's a money making scheme" or "you must have suffered an emotional trauma in order to get cancer"

She was a firm believer that food has a massive impact on healing. Now for me this has been slightly true and I firmly believe that what we put into our bodies can help us to get better but I do not believe it will heal me, only God can do that! Her comments landed on deaf ears thankfully but it did get me thinking... is this what I come across like because I believe God will heal me. Am I nutty?! Probably!

In some way I think I am, and I know people who think I am in denial because I am believing in something other than modern medicine. But in another way I believe that putting your trust in something like she has is the only way through this journey!

Now I wouldn't ever tell someone if you don't believe in my God you will probably die. So in a way we are nothing alike but I do like to let people know that in 'my' situation God will have the glory in this journey! I'm not afraid to stand up for what I believe in but I also would never push what I believe on someone in the way she did. We are all with our own opinions and beliefs. I'm just pleased she has something she can believe in so passionately!

Also I think for anyone who doesn't have a faith, her words would have floored you! It would have brought a lot crashing down around you, and I realised just simple praise for the God who loves me and is going to heal me from the inside out is needed from me! It is the best way to overcome someone else's comments like this.

Don't tell anyone but I actually prayed for her as she talked at me in the shop. Obviously not so she could hear but she really came across to me as someone who is lost and I love that we have a God that is always looking to bring His sheep within the loving embrace of His arms!

I am blessed to have something that is a continuous source of strength on this journey!

"Imagine the blessings we are missing simply because we thought our 'jobs' were more important than what He has to give us! Being patient and just sitting is tough if you are an 'on the go' person, but the rewards could be miraculous."
– *Laura Stephenson*

"Laura was always inspirational, challenging, positive and faith-filled. She was such an example and had such a positive impact on my life. At key points she spoke words of encouragement and truth. I'm so glad and privileged to have known her."

"Monday night running. Laura with the pram……. and still quicker than us!"

November 20th 2018   WOBBLES AND MESSAGES

In for chemo today and my blood cancer makers are still rising! Clearly they are like my lymph nodes and just haven't had Gods memo yet!

Now I am standing on the word and verses like Psalm 103:3 'He forgives all my sins and **heals** all my diseases' and this isn't just spiritual disease it includes physical ones too.

I had a little wobble I must admit, and messaged my amazing church ladies to let them know. Within a matter of minutes God has set to work reminding me that He sees my wobble and that He is **still** in this with me and He has given us the authority to say I am **healed**.

I had a message from someone that used the exact words I had prayed this morning on the way to work, *"Therefore, God elevated him to the place of highest honour and gave him the name above all other names,"* Philippians 2:9

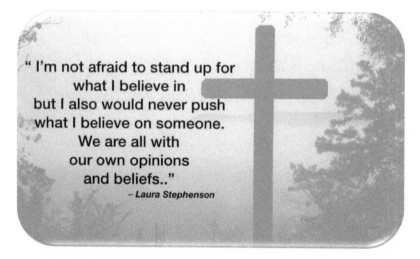

" I'm not afraid to stand up for what I believe in but I also would never push what I believe on someone. We are all with our own opinions and beliefs.."
– Laura Stephenson

And then a story was given to me to read, by a child with the most wonderful message for me

"But David kept going. It isn't how strong you are or how many swords and spears you have that will save you – it is God who saves you! This is God's battle. And God always wins his battles!"

There are no coincidences, and how anyone can deny that He is watching over me would be crazy! He loves his children way more than rubies and gold, and we must never forget that!

I praise His almighty name for never letting me forget this battle is won I need to fight, but He will have the glory when I am victorious!

December 9th 2018   A LESSON TO BE LEARNED

I haven't written in a while and it's not down to anything being wrong or worse! It's purely down to getting a virus (bound to happen with three girls!) so I have been ill in bed for a number of days plus it meant my bloods weren't quite right to have chemo on Monday which was a bit rubbish.

However, looking at it from a faith perspective (not my human response) I realised that maybe this could be a teaching lesson from God. When in doubt what does he want me to learn through this? For me I felt that God was teaching me, that sometimes it is about faith and receiving his word not relying on my five senses and how I feel about something. I have spent the past 15 rounds of chemo thinking great, my faith and these drugs are going to bring about my healing. But I think by not having it this week, I heard from God saying you only need me and the power inside you given by Jesus Christ! It is so easy to trust in human things that we can see but trusting completely in God is not as quick to be trusted! It did take me by surprise to be told sorry not this week, as my first thought was 'oh no it will grow' but that isn't true.

I believe I am healed and therefore my trust, belief and future is in his hands. Isaiah 58:8-9 says it perfectly,

"Then your salvation will come like the dawn, and your wounds will quickly heal. Your godliness will lead you forward, and the glory of the Lord will protect you from behind. Then when you call, the Lord will answer. 'Yes, I am here,' he will quickly reply."

I have as ever been so supported this week, when I had my bad thoughts (the enemy thinks he is being defeated and he is terrified!) my beautiful family and friends pull me through! I have so many like-minded people full of faith around me, I get so blessed hearing from them all!

I am learning not to live by my feelings but to live in total faith. It isn't always easy in this battle but it is always worth it! I will not live any other way through this battle. The Lord is my leader in this battle, and He has given me the **power** to receive my healing. I do not underestimate how powerful this is, and no wonder I have those bad thoughts. The enemy is terrified when I step more and more into my healing. Standing firm on the words that I have been given in the bible is the way through. I will not be swayed by negative thoughts. I will not be moved from what is promised to me and receiving it. As someone has just preached at church, holding onto His promises is the way forward, I know that not looking around at the situation which is a missed chemo week but at trusting full force in His **word** ! What a blessing it is!

Then when you call, the LORD will answer. "Yes, I am here," he will quickly reply. "Remove the heavy yoke of oppression. Stop pointing your finger and spreading vicious rumours!"

"She was wonderful to talk to and was a pleasure to be around."

"Chatting about allsorts whilst she was having Chemo via Facebook or Messenger. We lifted ourselves when we were all on our own."

"In Chemo today I have been blessed today with meeting some amazing people. It is incredible how kind people are when you are here, and what a difference it makes to your mind set! They will have no idea what a blessing they were to me today but it's very much appreciated!" *– Laura Stephenson*

December 10th 2018   PEOPLE WHO ARE THERE

Been here for 6 hours and no treatment ready! But never mind, onwards and upwards... no point having a whinge as every nurse is working so hard and it's not their fault they are absolute angels!

I have also been blessed today with meeting some amazing people, the couple sat next to me have kept jumping up to make me brews and make sure I had everything I needed; plus, we have talked for most of those six hours! Then I met a lady and her niece who again have chatted to me and cheered me up no end! Offering help whenever I need, just at the end of the phone line if I'm having a bad day, and a friend who has been there and is smiling out the other side of it saying the perfect things to keep me on the right side of my positive attitude!

It is incredible how kind people are when you are here, and what a difference it makes to your mind set! They will have no idea what a blessing they were to me today but it's very much appreciated!

A friend shared an article today and it really brought Christmas joy into my heart...

"These — and a thousand other promises — came true that first Christmas. And they assure us that God will keep every precious promise he's given us in his word."

December 24th 2018   INCREDIBLE HOW KIND.

I will share a few updates today. I'm sure whilst having chemo but this one really explores the truth of our celebrations at Christmas! Have a wonderful, happy, healthy Christmas!It is incredible how kind people are when you are here, and what a difference it makes to your mind set! They will have no idea what a blessing they were to me today but it's very much appreciated!

"This Christmas, don't let the world's misunderstanding of Christmas keep you from seeing and treasuring the greatest of all realities: God has been made low to bring us up.

Emmanuel has come to be with us. The promises have all come true."

Another chemo almost done...

I have been learning and listening to God while sat here today, no downloaded movie for me to watch, just chatting to those around me and reading my book. What has struck me more than anything is that we have no reason to fear.

The lady sat next to me today has been lovely, very chatty and full of medical and holistic knowledge which has been great. But at the centre of it all, whilst we have been chatting I have heard a lot of fear coming from her. In everything she has talked about, there has been an underlying note of fear and worry.

I've listened and tried to help alleviate those as best I can, and at times I probably understand how she feels; however, my overwhelming feeling is that I just want to give her what I have!

I want her to have what I have, that no fear or worry because I know there is a power in me that arrives on Christmas Day!

That then leads me on to the other side of things that God has been prompting me on. My healing is promised in His word but it also says it has already been given. That means it is mine, my body is healed. So I need my healing now to be manifested in my body. It's such a hard thing to get your head round, it doesn't get preached about often but as I see it I need to be thanking God for it, and asking for everything to be cleared out the way (including some of my thoughts) so that I can see that manifested healing in my body! My prayer life now needs to reflect that too!

I have so much on my side, why would I be anything but positive and full of joy! I just need to distribute that joy and fearless living out to others as much as I can! The enemy better be fearful because I am a lioness that will not stop.

51

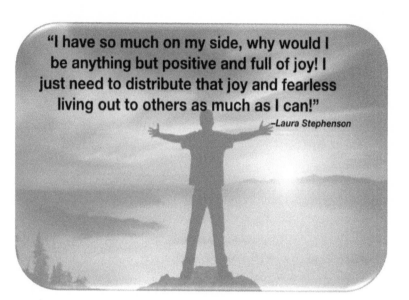

"I have so much on my side, why would I be anything but positive and full of joy! I just need to distribute that joy and fearless living out to others as much as I can!"

—Laura Stephenson

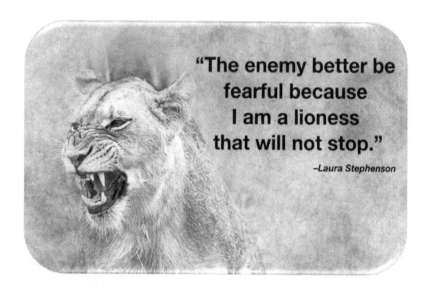

"The enemy better be fearful because I am a lioness that will not stop."

—Laura Stephenson

<u>December 31st 2018   WHAT A YEAR!!!</u>

I think this says it all about my last year... a tough year but also filled with some amazing goodness! 2019 looks set to be our best year yet! Love to you all and thank you for everything you have done for our family this year! You all make me smile and I can't wait to build more memories with you all in the many years ahead...

Well what a year!? As we head into 2019, I must reflect on what a tough year it has been. Life certainly threw me a curve ball. But 2019 will see complete healing and the restoration of every cell that shouldn't be behaving badly restored to its glory!

To say 2018 has been the worst year ever would be giving it the power. It's not been the worst year; it's just been tougher than others. But I am made of tough stuff, and there is no way I am letting anything other than my God have the power in this situation. That stupid C word does not have any power over my past year, nor will it in my year ahead.

2018 has ....

..... given me a beautiful 5-year-old who makes me laugh with her rapping, love of anything girlie and so many bonding memories;

...... given me the joy of watching my one-year-old twins play together, make me laugh and see their love of adventure grow much to my horror sometimes!

...... made me realise how close I am now to my incredible husband, the one man who is stronger than I ever imagined and I would be lost without!

…….. grown my bond with my family that have tirelessly and selflessly cooked, cleaned, ironed and generally just been there through everything in the last year. They are the glue to so many amazing times, and I can't wait to make a million more with them all.

…….. made me realise how many amazing friends and adopted family, as I like to term them, I have and just how precious they are to me with their words, meals, gifts, and helping me day to day.

Finally, 2018 has given me a huge push, head first, into a deeper relationship with God. I am his daughter, a princess to a king and one of His most precious children. It has been so exciting to journey this with my faith growing massively every day.

To know that whilst sometimes it looks like a storm is raging around me, the winds have picked up and the waves are getting higher; the boat I am in will not falter, capsize or even sustain a dent because I am protected, secure and steadfast on the words of God that say

"I have the victory in this and He is my rear guard" (Isaiah 58:8)

If I have been taught anything in 2018, it's that life isn't fair but I have a God who loves me so much that He will not let me fail. He will raise me up, and in His word I can fully **trust**. I have no fear in 2019 because I have a God that has not given me the spirit of fear but of love, peace and a sound mind! Also there are a few words in that big book called the bible that tell me, **I am healed and I have the victory**!

So 2019 will be an amazing year of restoration, renewal and growth!! Bring it on!

Happy New Year to you all and a huge thank you for everything you have done for me in 2018! The prayers alone mean the world to me and I love that I stand side by side with so many of you in my faith that God has the victory in this situation already!

"Your beautiful smile Laura, lit up the playground. Your laughter and sense of humour was infectious. Your bravery and positivity were amazing."

"What a legacy of of positivity, strength, hope and faith you've left. I'm a busy tired mum, just like you but today has made me remember to take time to sit at our Lord's feet; be thankful, be hopeful and share."

"When Laura spoke to you she looked you in the eyes and asked, "How are you?" and she truly meant it. What an inspiration she was to us all."

January 16th 2019   RUBBISH START BUT

So today had a really rubbish start, if I'm being honest I think sometimes as humans we let the weight of the world build up around us and weigh heavy on our hearts and souls. It's a natural thing to have these days in life in general never mind when you are faced with facts that tell you you should be worried or scared because facts in a world perspective are truth.

As ever I have had some amazing people alongside me today boosting me up and giving me those messages from God that take my faith to a different level. It's been a day for letting others faith step forward in strength where I haven't had the strength to do it.

God did speak to me though this afternoon, as I drove home the heavens opened and the hail, that proceeded to hit my car, was incredible. I watched the white hail build up on my car and listened to the deafening sound of it hitting the roof and windscreen. It was loud and scary. But I had the protection of my car, and I would get home and be ok.

"YOUR STRENGTH WILL COME FROM SETTLING DOWN IN **COMPLETE DEPENDENCE** ON ME."

ISAIAH 30V15 MSG

In that moment I realised that God wanted me to see that the world and our worries sometimes feels like a hail storm, it's loud and scary. But His Word is our protection. It says countless times 'do not fear' or 'do not be afraid' so we need to take note of that because if it's mentioned more than once it must be pretty important in our walk with Him!

It doesn't mean we won't have fears because we are human after all but it does mean that when we do, we can look to 1 Peter 5:7 and cast our fears onto Him because he cares for us more than we could **ever** imagine.

"Sometimes as humans we let the weight of the world build up around us and weigh heavy on our hearts and souls. It's a natural thing to have these days in life in general, never mind when you are faced with facts that tell you you should be worried or scared."

– Laura Stephenson

"Through her trouble, she never seemed to grumble or moan. May her life of positivity remain in each of us."

January 19th 2019   WHAT A PAIN!

The past few days I have been plagued with a pain in the top of my hip going round to my back. It's not been horrendous, just a constant source of pain, which can be so distracting. It has stopped me from doing things with my girls. It's not the worst thing but it has been annoying.

From the start I have known that God is in all my situations, gently creating a path through the wilderness as it says in Isaiah 43:19. Yesterday I listened again to a video on fear and how standing on the word of God is the only way through anything we face. Therefore, prayers have been about the power of Jesus taking away this pain. If he can part the Red Sea what is my little pain?!

This morning I have woken up with very little pain, and by the end of the day I know it will be gone completely. When we face anything if we have the word of God to stand on, what can we not face?! We can take on illness and any scheme the enemy throws at us!

Whatever you are facing don't forget that our God is above all. His name is higher than anything and we are sons and daughters of the most high king... who have we to fear?!

All glory to Him! It's no coincidence that my pain is gone! #prayerworks

January 27th 2019   HOPE AND .... A PROMISE

Singing this morning at church and again God brings me to this image with its words across the front.

I think recently I have been a bit anxious about my body. What is this horrible poison (which is playing its part) doing to those healthy cells in my body and my other organs.

I see side effects, my skin coming off because it's so dry, my fingers splitting and losing taste buds. I am as ever amazed at how my body is taking each and every shot of chemo, He truly made me perfectly! Yet it is being tested to a great extreme.

Despite all of this I have a been given a HOPE; an assurance, and a PROMISE that this will end. It isn't forever & His word promises me that I am healed. People find it really hard to understand how you can believe in something that you can't see or be confident in, yet every day we believe in love because we can feel it for those around us. I didn't choose this path but I will trust in Him through it all because I can't imagine this journey relying on human wisdom rather than His higher power.

I have been surround by some amazing people; they lift me when I need it, they encourage, listen, be positive & share my passion for His glory to be seen in this situation! I love these people I'm doing life with! They have no idea how much they mean to me, and just what a huge blessing they are in my life. Regardless of where they live or how different our lives may appear we are connected by His love and His word! Just amazing!

In the next few weeks I have another scan to see what's happening, and I have my 20th round of chemo! Lots of anxieties come up but I know that my trust is in something steadfast that PROMISES healing so what have I got to fear! Absolutely nothing! Prayer to see my healing manifested would be amazing. Thank you

February 1st 2019   GUESS WHAT !!

As ever never a dull moment with this path I'm on... This week has been a bit testing as I was told I needed to have urgent bloods taken because my kidneys weren't functioning as they should be. Despite not being aware of this I did what they asked me to do and drank dutifully my two litres of water a day. As many of you may understand water to me is boring (someone has suggested a great alternative to make it livelier so I will be testing that out this week) but for a day and a half I drank two litres to be ready for the bloods to show my kidneys were functioning well.

A day and a half worth of water was not going to massively change the results of that I am certain, so I jumped on my phone to my trusted church ladies and asked for them to stand with me asking God to make the difference.

And guess what He did!

I have just heard back that my bloods for my kidneys are back to normal levels! It had been such a worry to me, what if my recent back ache was because of them or if they were failing under the pressure of so much chemo! I wouldn't have been surprised if that was the case. However, I have always maintained that my body was created perfectly; psalm 139;14! So this body falls under His creations and will continue to work as He intended.

Why do we worry and fear things out of our control, when we have a God that can work His power for our good in all things? I trust Him in all of this and I need to trust that when things come up (which they inevitably will) I will give them back to Him and trust that He will resolve it all.

This has given me a real wake up call. His healing is being manifested in my body, throughout. And as a good friend said to me today; Luke 10:19. He has given us the power to commend these things to not harm us. It is in Jesus living in us that we can have authority over schemes that set to cause us harm.

I will be raising so many Hallelujahs for this blessing! (Listen to "Raise a hallelujah" by Bethel if you haven't already) it is my anthem song suggested by another wonderful lady in this battle!
I have a scan on Sunday, I have not been given a spirit of fear (Timothy) about it but know that I want to ask God again to show those doctors just how powerful He is! I have no doubt in Him! If you could pray (if it's your thing) that would be amazing thank you everyone

60

"People find it really hard to understand how you can believe in something that you can't see or be confident in, yet everyday we believe in love because we can feel it for those around us. .."

– Laura Stephenson

"Why do we worry and
fear things are out
of our control
when we have a God
that can work
His power for our good
in all things.
I trust Him in all of this"

–Laura Stephenson

February 6th 2019   AN INTERESTING DAY

Today was an in interesting day! I had chemo and sat next to a guy I have met before with the same cancer as me and we had a good chat!

I had a wonderful dinner made for me by Inglewhite Church again! (They are beyond kind in the meals we get!) I'd be lost without their prayers and love at the moment.

Finally, God placed me in a position to speak to a friend, who is asking a lot of questions about life at the moment. Questions I have asked many times, and also ones that I believe God has given me answers too just for this lady. In all of this that I am going through, it is easy to wonder why me, but despite it I am being called to talk about my faith, healing and this amazing God that I have. He is calling me to be that person to others, and His glory will shine through my healing in this situation I find myself in.

I don't have all the answers but I serve a God that does!

As I was deciding I should fight my chemo awake brain and head to sleep God prompted me to read my bible plan for today. The devotional

His presence, His love, overwhelmed me. It hurt him that I was walking through suffering. I am still awed at the moment. I heard Psalm 23 loud and clear within in me—though you walk through the shadow of the valley of death. I would walk through. This was a shadow. He would be with me.

Was I still tired? Did I still feel pain? Yes and yes. But oh, in that precious moment of worship, God's love washed over me and inside me. I believe that in that experience I could truly say with Job, "Though He slay me, yet will I trust Him" Job 13:15 (NKJV).

is here; the words tell a story but are so incredibly similar to His voice talking to me it made me laugh out loud (a little bad with Mark asleep next to me) he didn't wake though.

Night all xx

February 11th 2019   TO SHARE OR NOT TO SHARE

I find that some weeks I have nothing to write, well nothing that I think is very interesting anyway... other weeks I feel fit to burst to tell people just what I think God is talking to me about. Now this change in action isn't because I particularly feel God is only talking to me on a schedule of every few weeks but I think down to me and my capacity to share.

Some weeks I feel like sharing and some days I don't. Now I will never be one of those people who doesn't over share because that's just how I was created! (much to Mark's sometimes discomfort at me discussing my toiletry habits!) but I also know that sometimes just being quiet and still is the best way to move forward.

Last week was a bit of a kicker for me as my results weren't exactly what I had been hoping for. There has been some growth and it therefore means my drugs need to change. As ever this isn't a huge blow, it's just a setback in this thing we are battling. There are options but ultimately I am back to fighting this head on and taking the full power of authority I have been given to tell this cancer where to go in His name!

But some days it's tiring. For a while now I have felt this overwhelming urge to fight, to battle and to declare that this is not taking me anywhere. And whilst that is (I still believe) the best way through this,

I have been reminded tonight, as I sat in bed reading an incredible blog by another lady battling just as hard as me and trusting in God with all she has, that sometimes it's ok to be honest with God. To tell him that you hate this situation, to cry and to curl up while you process how rubbish you feel with it all. We are in a relationship with God, warts and all, and if it was a relationship with a friend or family member we would let them see the good and the bad, the tears and the laughter, so we need to do the same with God.

63

Letting my guard down with God, is not the same as me saying I don't think I'll be healed or I don't trust Him. It actually just brings me closer to Him, as the father that loves me and wants to take care of me. My faith deepens as I open up more to Him by not pretending that I am ok all the time.

Sometimes it's ok to not be 'fine' that's when I think we find our closest moments to the God that protects, holds, and comforts us. It's in those moments we see a beauty to our relationship with him that we have never seen before. God doesn't want us to have a surface level relationship with Him but one that is so deep that we are refined and transformed at the end of it all. It isn't always easy, but He will never forsake us or leave us empty handed.

Trust in Him. Lean on Him. He is a good God.

February 17th 2019   A HUMAN EMOTION

Today I have been silly busy (I have most of this weekend with Mark being away!) but secretly I have loved having time just me with my girls. They are such a source of joy and amaze me with how clever and loving they are.

At the back of my mind though has been the constant thought, Tuesday is change day. Now that's not necessarily a bad thing but it is launching me again into an unknown territory of new drugs and new side effects. My body is 'fearfully and wonderfully made' so I must not doubt that He has made it to withstand more than I can possibly imagine. Despite what is in there that doesn't belong, it is still created spectacularly by Him.

YOU ARE
INFINITELY
more loved
THAN YOU EVER DARED DREAM

He didn't give me this cancer and He will take my body back to all He intended it to be when I was created.

Fear is a human emotion, and one that we should feel. There is no shame in being fearful, no guilt in it and it doesn't mean we don't believe in miracles! But I refuse to sit in the middle of fear and stay there! Yes I have been fearful because again I am out of control of this next step. But when will I learn that this is not mine to control. I face that fear and I tell it to go. I have not been given a spirit of fear!

In all of this I have come to realise that God loves me. Now that's a pretty standard thing for a Christian to say. It's no new thing that we believe we are loved by God; I mean He sent his only son to die for us. But the enormity of how much He loves us I don't think we truly grasp. God loves little old me beyond anything I can imagine. Take how much I love my girls and mark and multiply it by 100 and it still doesn't come close.

So if I truly believe He loves me that much then how could I doubt that He isn't holding my hand right now in that fear and dragging me out to stand on His word.   He is angry at the situation and He will fight for me, see my healing complete and wrap me up when I feel fearful.

If it was just me or you on this planet, He would still have sent His only son to die for you simply because we make Him smile. We were designed for great things and He loves us! So with that in mind, a father who loves us that much and is fighting a battle for us what chance does fear have!

Those who do please pray for me this week, that my body shows those doctors just what it is made of, that the healing starts to wow them and that they are equipped and pumped up enough to guide me in the medical stuff!

"She showed so many a way to walk through the trials and difficulties of life; she showed them how to be a friend and how to love. She has left a permanent impression on so many people."

"I, for one, will always endeavour to be 'More Lol', to live in the moment; to feel each experience and embrace life with mindful positivity and gratitude."

Her love of Frosties, Cola sweets and Dawson's Creek, to her fierce loyalty and depth of friendship. What I remember most of all though is her love for you all. I don't think I've ever known anyone to have such a pride in her family as Laura.

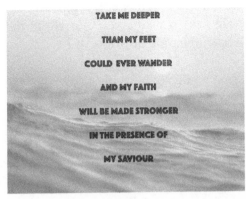

TAKE ME DEEPER

THAN MY FEET

COULD EVER WANDER

AND MY FAITH

WILL BE MADE STRONGER

IN THE PRESENCE OF

MY SAVIOUR

New drugs; new day! And not such a bad day, but I am not surprised as every time I step into that place God just introduces me to new things and thoughts. Today I met a lovely girl, and God caught my attention with her as we share the same date for our birthday and she is a twin. I really feel that God wanted to teach me about exploring some other options at the Christie and boy did He talk to me about that today.

I have been told that the side effects of this drug can be a bit scary, it can give my vocal cords a spasm which will make me feel like I can't breathe and my throat is closing up, I will need to wear gloves for the fridge and go down a freezer aisle on the supermarket will hurt me too. But I walked out of that centre and felt no pain... I am under no illusion that it might happen or I might feel something different but my hair may grow back, my skin may go back to normal and I am still fighting so what is there to worry about!

These drugs are effective, and yes they have nasty side effects but I stand before them and tell them to flee. I don't want you thanks very much!

Your mind is an incredible thing, so rather trusting my feelings I trust my mind to sort my body out and get it to line up with my way of thinking, with health, and with healing.

Thank you for all of your love, care and kindness in this. You are wonderful people! I would be lost without you! Stay amazing because you make people's lives brighter!

February 27th   SOME DAYS ARE TOUGH AND OTHERS …

This week (it's only Wednesday) has been a tough one. But in it all I am reminded that the Lord sees me, He sees my situation and He is not content to sit back and let these things break me down.

I had treatment last week (new drugs) and have been blessed by God to not experience many side effects. I was told some scary stuff about side effects before I left treatment and yet I walked out of Rosemere feeling as good as when I went in. Now don't get me wrong I am not saying that I won't feel these side effects at some time but at the moment I'm the same. So I trust in these words: -

"I will never fail you or disappoint you. My promises are rainbows of hope that cover you. My declarations over your life are greater than your heartache. Your tears are liquid words that I read and understand. Never doubt My conquering love, for I have determined to build you up into a spiritual house filled with trust, hope, and love."

Lord God, you know all my desires and my deepest longings. My tears are liquid words and you can read them all. **Psalm 38:9**

March 3rd 2019   JUST A KISS

This week I couldn't have chemo, my neuts (better known as the immune system part of my body) decided to be too low and although it is annoying I would rather that than risk sepsis (which is a possibility if I went ahead with chemo) It's not a great result but at the end of the day I have to trust that God knows best and although it sucks to think I'm not tackling this, it reminds me who is in control!

I did want to share what happened whilst I was sat in the chemo unit waiting for my blood results to come back. ……… I sat across from a couple. The lady was probably my age; she wore a blue head scarf as she had obviously lost her hair. There was a sick container in front of her and she was trying to sleep while her chemo took place. Next to her sat her husband. God asked me to pray for this lady, so I did. I sat in the hustle and bustle where I was and asked God to take care of her.

A minute later I watched her husband lean forward and kiss the top of her forehead.

In that moment I heard God tell me that, despite how I might feel or worry, He has not gone anywhere. He is kissing my forehead in the same way that husband kissed his wife. He is a constant in my life when things seem to be ever changing and I have bad news, He will not forsake me or leave me. It was a real light bulb moment, I knew the Lord was talking to me and the message was so clear.

If He is for me, who can be against me!

Have a good weekend everyone.

March 10ᵗʰ 2019   A COMMUNITY

This morning I have been reminded that we are a community. We all crave belonging, acceptance and community. It's a love that we all need in our lives.

For many of us this comes from those around us, but for me it also comes from our relationship with God. In His arms we find all of the things we crave as humans.

This journey for me I think has taught me so much already. Not only has it taught me to read my bible more often and to trust in His word but it has also shown me how much I rely and value the communities I belong too.

I have an amazing group of ladies and gents who time after time include me in their prayers. They don't include me in their prayers because it is what they are meant to do, they don't feel obligated to pray for me and they certainly don't do it because they think for one moment that I am doomed in all of this!

They do it because I am part of their community. That community is not confined by four walls. It isn't defined by the time we spend together and it isn't limited to a certain number of miles.

Community is one that promotes love, cares for each other no matter the distance, allows you to be vulnerable and never gets annoyed when someone asks to be remembered in prayer.

God wants us in community and our enemy wants us isolated

Surround yourself with people who make you hungry for life, touch your heart and nourish your soul,

encourage each other and build each other up

anon

Home is ultimately not about a place to live but about the people with whom you are most fully alive . Home is about love, relationship community and belonging and we are all searching for home
Erwin McManus

I could not do this journey without the secret, often in the background, people that surround me. It is those people who quietly pray for me, quietly give me a hug when I need it or quietly offer up thoughts to boost me despite the miles between us.

We are invited into a community continually everyday by God. He sent Jesus to us to invite us in to this amazing community knowing that it is what our hearts crave and it is what we need here on earth when going through a battle or just living a life full of blessings.

So whatever your communities; know that it is ok to not be independent but to rely on those around you. It doesn't make you weak, it actually makes you stronger than you could ever imagine. With that and Gods word what could possibly stand against us. Thank you my communities that are friends for all your prayers, love and support! I'd be lost without you and my faith.

"I love these people I'm doing
life with!
They have no idea how much
they mean to me, and just what
a huge blessing they are in my
life." *– Laura Stephenson*

"It is ok to not be
independent
but to rely on those around
you.
It doesn't make you weak,
it actually makes you
stronger
than you could ever
imagine."
– Laura Stephenson

"I'll always remember her saying 'I accept the diagnosis but not the prognosis!" There's no doubt that she was a remarkable woman and fighter."

There is so much to be celebrated in the beauty and strength of Laura's life and the legacy she leaves in her girls. My life is better for knowing her and having her as a true friend throughout our time at Runshaw and Longton

CHOOSE TO BE POSITIVE

Today has been interesting to say the least; that and emotional. I think I forget how much all of this takes out of me, not only is it having an effect on my body but it has an effect on my emotions too.

It's ok to say that and it certainly doesn't make me weak or ill.

I have my moment and then I pull up my big girl pants, face those fears or stresses of my week. Grab my strength and tackle it all head on ready to battle again. I am bigger than this; I won't stand for negativity, I say no to labels and I am still just 'Laura'. My day started with not knowing what was happening in terms of treatment and had a bit of knockback before leaving for the hospital, so along came the emotions! Thankfully my husband and parents came to my rescue. I gave blood (which had to be checked again as my neuts were still low) and then headed for lunch with dad to await the phone call to find out if I could have chemo this week.

Lots of prayers later and I got the wonderful phone call to say I could have chemo. Then I waited for drugs to be ready, and bumped into the lovely lady I had met the time before. Such a joy to chat to her and give her a hug.

Chemo started at 4pm, and once again I met a new lovely lady. The lady I met was the same lady that I had mentioned in my previous post all about the kiss of God. She happened to be in the same room as me (I don't like being in a room normally so they move me but they didn't today) and I mentioned that she had inspired a previous post! From that we talked non-stop until I left at 6.30.

It was so lovely meeting her, such a positive lady going through some horrendous side effects but all with a smile. We shared the fact that sometimes it's ok to feel low, unsure or emotional. We are allowed to be vulnerable as long as we don't stay there and we keep pushing forward!

As I left, the first lot of side effects from this new drug for me kicked in. I got hit by the cold and my fingertips (every one of them) suddenly had the worst pins and needles I've ever had. They lasted for a long time after I got in the car, but as always I prayed over them. Thank you for letting me feel things God but you can control these side effects for me; and then I sang worship songs all the way home and by the time I arrived home it had all gone!

Finally, this picture just captures my attitude today. Have a good week, be positive (it's a choice) and stay strong! We have a power we can trust to bring healing, miracles and compassion!

A strong person
is not the one
that doesn't cry
A strong person
is the one
who
cries and sheds
tears for a moment,
then gets up
and fights again

"It has been a privilege to watch Laura grow up into the incredible, beautiful and inspirational young woman she became."

"We have watched Laura grow and live her life, making the best of opportunities. We have admired her resolute manner, her care and dedication to her family and her unquestioning belief in God. These and many more strengths have enabled her to conduct her life in such a way that we have all learnt from her."

"What a ray of sunshine she was, even at 11 years old; so caring and always smiling."

This week has been a week of **joy**, which may sound like a strange thing to say when in the midst of a storm like I am. But I don't think our circumstances should define our feelings. We make a choice each day how we approach the things we face and the things that surround us. I'm not saying it's easy or pain free but I have found that it melts fear and stress away - *Psalm 63:7*

This verse has been at the front of my mind over the last few weeks, Isaiah 43;19. It talks about new things and this has been my situation this week. I am starting some new things to help in this next stage of my journey. I have the opportunity to have some new medication, household medication with very little side effects which will weaken the naughty cells in my body and allow the chemo to attack it better! It is exciting and I feel like my fight has been encouraged The positivity I found in this consultant was fantastic, He understood me and is so encouraging.   He isn't promising my healing (I already have that from Him) but he is wanting me to be encouraged by their research and others stories

In this new stage I have had a lot of 'side thoughts' (I know where they have come from) and they aren't God thoughts. I have let myself be taken into that thought arena and was given the picture of a bull fighting ring. Me in the middle ready to face these thoughts entering the ring with power and determination. When we have new positive blessings enter our lives, the enemy wants to counter them and comes at us not quietly and with a soft approach but with a power so full and determined to throw us off course. Don't be fooled that it will be softly softly but be prepared and on your toes to dance out of the way and defeat that bull.

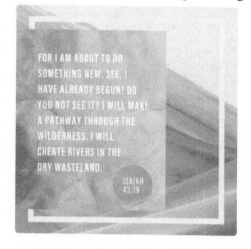

FOR I AM ABOUT TO DO SOMETHING NEW. SEE, I HAVE ALREADY BEGUN! DO YOU NOT SEE IT? I WILL MAKE A PATHWAY THROUGH THE WILDERNESS. I WILL CREATE RIVERS IN THE DRY WASTELAND.
ISAIAH 43:19

The way I have defeated it and waved my red flag this week was through JOY. It is the fastest way to take down those bulls that charge towards us. It totally removes the power in those thoughts, it isn't easy but I would rather destroy them than be controlled by them!

Another thing that keeps cropping up this week is 'under his wings'. Now doesn't this sound like an idyllic safe place to be?! Nothing can get to you and you can just be still. I kind of imagine that it is a soft blanket under a tree, with your favourite book and complete silence to just relax. I have been challenged this week to also understand that under his wings is all of that but it is also somewhere that you can battle or fight. There is a protection there but there is also the opportunity to battle from that position.

We should always be ready to battle, find that strength to take up a sword and stand firm. It is going to take patience but it also takes joy and trust.

April 2ⁿᵈ 2019   A SEASON OF CHANGE

In this season of change, restoration and renewal God has been talking to me about it being finished or case closed. I really feel that in all of this the promises are there, and God is showing me that with water and reflection those seeds planted will come to fruition because it is **done**. A dear friend has been blessing me immensely for the last 40 days by recording a prayer for me each day, which I get sent to listen too as I start my day. What I have loved most about this blessing is that it is rooted in scripture, every day I have been blessed with a different bible verse. I have verses that I have read over the years and they have revealed a new character to the good God I know as well as verses that I never knew existed. In all of this I am listening to different blogs, videos and pastors; it has really opened my eyes to different theories and blessings. This spoke to me last week and I really hope it blesses you. We are never without Hope.

"Strength isn't found on the mountain tops but in the climb. Drought and fires, though painful, draw the strength of God out of you that no other situation in your life can, fires burn away the old to make room for the new.

77

*Drought causes your complete and utter dependency upon the Father.
God doesn't create the drought and fires, but He will use them to build
a resilience in you that you never knew you had. A resilience and
strength that you will need to walk into the promises He has for you.
Why? Because God has called you to influence, not to cower and
influence requires strength. You may have been cowering through the
fires, but you will walk out with the spiritual muscles of Samson. I
declare over you this day, the drought you have been in, the seemingly
endless barren wasteland, it has been broken. You have been declared
a drought-free zone. The rains are washing over you and your family
this very moment. What was difficult will be broken as it's replaced
with the fruits and flowers of an abundant spring "*

NATE+CHRISTY JOHNSTON

I am strong but I am only strong in His strength. It isn't about me, or
down to me doing anything differently it is all in His strength. And when
the final case is revealed in my life God will have the glory!

Be blessed this week, walk in His strength and know that if we trust in
Him those things that bring us down can be a case closed situation.

April 2nd 2019   TREATMENT

So what is happening with me, treatment wise; in all of this I am
focusing on my faith because I know it is what brings my healing but
equally I have to go through the fires on this journey.

The last lot of chemo is taking its toll on me in terms of being more tired
than normal, and the side effects are more prominent than the last lot of
drugs. I could manage losing my hair as it is something I knew would
return at some point. This time round I am at risk of neuropathy which
could be irreversible if it is left to get worse. The only thing they could
do is reduce my dosage so that it doesn't get too bad, but as you can
imagine I don't want that to happen. I want to fight this with all I have
and can cope with side effects. Although it was difficult trying to blow
the twins nose the other day or trying to undo their jacket zip, the
neuropathy means that my hands spasm and won't respond to what my
brain is telling them to do. On top of that my vocal cords spasm and

it feels as if something is lodged at the back of my throat when I try to swallow or eat. When I get cold, my hands get pins and needles, which can be fun!

In all of this I know that the chemo is working to fight this thing, I want to use it but I also want to protect my other healthy organs (I have **some** working properly.

I have it a lot easier than others I have met, and if God is for me ...

But if you do, please pray that the neuropathy would be limited so I don't have to reduce my dosage, that the healthy organs and cells would be allowed to prosper and that the new drugs I am taking alongside my chemo weaken those nasty cells to have more of a positive impact.

Thank you guys.

> "There are times when I am quite frankly tired. I am strong but some days I want to rest my head and shout at the world that I don't want to be in this situation.."
> – *Laura Stephenson*

This is part of the stuff supporting my body in this process. Notice I am not saying it will cure me (Only God can heal me) but boy does it help me.

So what do we have here; we have apricot kernels (yes they contain cyanide but limit how many I take a day), vitamin D and vitamin K (good for my bones), milk thistle (good to cleanse the liver of toxins), turmeric (just a great root!), asparagus juice (really great at killing those cells that aren't doing their job), smoothie (antioxidant so great at flushing out those nasties).

And then come my new drugs, which aren't a trial they are from a private clinic but one which I have heard great things about.

Diabetic tablets - stop those naughty cells getting any sugar for energy; Cholesterol tablets - break down the hard shell that is created around the naughty cells and make them visible again to my own immune system, Tape worm tablets (yes you heard right?!?) - these make the cells weak, like us not having water in the desert Antibiotics - target the stem cells that cause spread

This weekend I was led to a post that really made me think. It mentioned that often the fullest rain clouds are almost black and very dark. And yet those clouds bring the rain. They bring something that promotes new life, encourages it and washes away the dead plants or leaves.

What an amazing image. What an amazing promise. My rain clouds have been dark but the winds of change are causing those clouds to break and release the best rain storm I have ever seen and for that I give **all** the glory to God!

"Today I saw a challenge and decided to face it with positivity. It was a choice to face it that way."

– *Laura Stephenson*

So in chemo again today, and once again I am amazed at just how God is using all of this for His glory! In the middle ground I find myself in, surrounded by a situation not of my creation or His, He gently reminds me that I am not alone and I can have a wonderful impact on those around me. I have once again met a lovely couple, and as usual the person sat next to me has the same diagnosis as me. This has happened so many times to me, that it almost becomes funny. It's no coincidence that I am sat next to someone who is in the same boat as me.

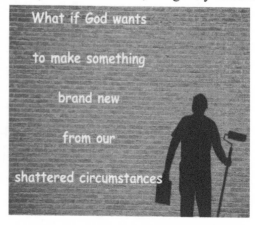

It has made me think about community. It can be a lonely place that only a select group understand the ins and outs of it all. That causes isolation and loneliness. But what if we looked at those negative feelings and asked them to leave. What would happen if we approach that select group with the intentions to add these people into our story! Imagine the impact we could have if we were open, honest and shared our story with others. We could maybe bring light into so many lives. How exciting that would be and what a privilege!

I was led in my book to the story of David, and how out of his situation he realised that he had to come back to God in repentance. God is still working. God still has a plan. God was still moulding and shaping David for a wonderful purpose - not just for him but to help others.
God didn't give me cancer, nor did my life choices cause it. But while I am in this middle ground awaiting a miracle I love that I can see His hand on my life. He is preparing me for my miracle and what a privilege it is to speak about my story in this place.

"Today I got to enjoy my girls and my time with them. Nothing stopped me or got in my way, and for someone going through this crazy journey that is simply the best feeling in the world! I wasn't poorly, I was Mummy."

—Laura Stephenson

"We played, we laughed and we enjoyed being together. It would be so easy to let treatment or my diagnosis get in the way of having this time or being a mummy"

– Laura Stephenson

"Your girls will be so proud of you in the years to come."

"What a wonderful mum she was; nothing too much trouble and never raising her voice."

"We both had twins. She made me feel so positive and full of happiness. I was lucky she came into mine and my children's lives."

Today was amazing. This last week I have had some negative thoughts, as ever I know that they do not not come from the God that I believe in. He does not give a spirit of fear!

But today made me realise that I can do all things through Him that gives me strength.

I took the girls to the Sea Life Centre in Manchester and then we went for lunch and a quick shop in the Trafford centre. I have never done anything like that before on my own, and recently the new chemo drugs have really taken 'it' out of me. I have tried to explain it's a type of tiredness that isn't about me not having enough sleep (although if honest I could go to bed earlier!!) it's simply as if my body just says I have no oomph (technical term)!

Taking three under 6 to something like that would have filled me with dread before being diagnosed. Today I saw a challenge and decided to face it with positivity. It was a choice to face it that way, to look at how I felt this morning (better than the end of last week) and say let's have a good fun filled day.

And that we did... we played, we laughed and we enjoyed being together. It would be so easy to let treatment or my diagnosis get in the way of having this time or being a mummy. Today I got to be the mummy that I always aim to be. I got to enjoy my girls and my time with them. Nothing stopped me or got in my way, and for someone going through this crazy journey that is simply the best feeling in the world! I wasn't poorly, I was Mummy.

And maybe the message that He is trying to get through to me is, 'Rest in Me when you need too and only then will you experience the BEST I have for you'.

In His strength I am **not** ill... I am **healed**! With all of that said some days it isn't easy being a parent, if they haven't had enough sleep or are hungry you can be fighting a losing battle with them. But today my girls behaved beautifully and it definitely would not have been the day it was without them just being so wonderful! Heidi helped me by watching her sisters while I ran to get high chairs, they all held hands and walked round together and best of all they made each other giggle. I am incredibly blessed by my daughters, and cannot wait to make decades of memories with them!

#iamhealed #ichoosetobepositive #inHisstrength

April 15ᵗʰ 2019   **GAME OF THRONES**

Watching Game of Thrones with my wonderful husband.   The opening scene made me smile. The queen makes her way into the castle in the north. The locals look at her with such hostility and contempt. Then her dragons come into view and fly over her and the crowds. A little smile spreads over her face.

Tonight it made me realise that this is the type of power I have behind me. I am surrounded on all sides by what appears to be a hopeless situation. And yet I am the daughter to a king, riding into the future with a smile on my face because I **know** the power I have behind me.

April 19ᵗʰ 2019   **THE CROSS**

This year this cross has more significance to me than ever before. He died on that cross for me; to forgive all my sins and to **heal** me. He took on the sins of the world. It was dark and then the son of the world lit up the darkness so that there would be no more if we make that choice to follow Him. I truly believe that through my journey His glory will be shown; bringing light into  what seems like a horrendous dark situation. I have that assurance of His love for me because I can have faith of what happened on that cross. I know that Jesus will work within my body making all of my cells align into the perfect way that they were created. He will not leave me wanting and His work has already begun. What a testimony of His work my body will be. How many more people will look to that cross at the end of all of this! Thank you Lord Jesus for all you are doing and for all that is to come. #goodfriday

April 23ʳᵈ 2019   THE WAY FORWARD

Today was chemo day. As always I was sat with someone who has the same diagnosis as me. Once again I believe this is no coincidence. While I am in this place I am being able to speak about my faith and what I believe is the best way forward in all of this.

How our bodies often mirror what our mind is saying. How we tackle this thing inside us that doesn't belong. How we look it in the eye and tell it that we will not be beaten. Yes, we all have our fearful days, our days of being human. It is something that should happen. We have to allow ourselves to feel that feeling but equally as I always say it is important not to let that feeling take over or to sit alongside it and have tea with it. (And that is not an easy path or easy for me to say) it is a fact but it is not truth.

"Fear is a human emotion, and one that we should feel. There is no shame in being fearful, no guilt in it and it doesn't mean we don't believe in miracles! But I refuse to sit in the middle of fear and stay there!"
— Laura Stephenson

"I pull up my big girl pants, face those fears or stresses of my week. Grab my strength and tackle it all head on, ready to battle again" — Laura Stephenson

God did not give us a spirit of fear but of love, power and a sound mind. So let's grab on to that when we feel broken down to dust and ask to be built back up into a beautiful vase of clay.

Another image I keep getting is rains that bring with them the new life of spring. Where things have been taking a stronghold and strangling the good; like weeds that spread and kill as they move this rain will paralyse them in their tracks. You know that fresh smell you get of cut grass when it has been warm and the rains finally arrive; that is how it will be with my healing. It will start in the place where the pains started when I was diagnosed, travel putting those bad weeds out of that I have no doubt. So I will pick up my sword and continue to terrify the enemy as I stand firm on the promises in the word.

With all of that said I have very recently felt very much under attack from all sides. When I say attacked; I don't mean literally but I mean that I have had more fearful days than normal; I am tired more often of having to fight this battle and I have been letting the world influence how I feel and react to things. This is when I realise that something is trying to derail the positivity and stance that I have, but it is also when I realise that I am walking in the right direction. God is pleased with me because I am listening to His voice. The picture explains it better than I can.

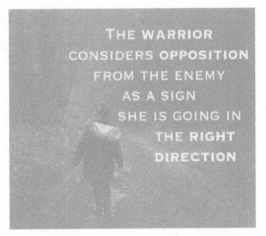

THE WARRIOR CONSIDERS OPPOSITION FROM THE ENEMY AS A SIGN SHE IS GOING IN THE RIGHT DIRECTION

The enemy is firing arrows at me on all sides and I will stand firm on His word. I know that my positivity, His power, and me standing on the word of God whilst praising Him for my healing is terrifying to the enemy. I am headed in the right direction and there is nothing that will stop me.

"To be a part of Laura's journey has been a privilege and an honour ……I always wished there was more we could do, but we were always made to feel we had done our best. I will raise a glass to celebrate what a beautiful and inspirational lady Laura was……… she never failed to see the positive side of life and that she will always be remembered for!"

"I'll always remember Laura in many amazing ways with a gorgeous smile and an amazing heart."

Yesterday was a draining day; I had a swelling in my neck around a lymph node. I know this lymph node is probably infected but I wanted to make sure my PICC line hadn't moved so in I went to the hospital.

I really dislike hospitals as many of us do. I feel like they are filled with doom and a sense of hopelessness (not the combination you want when you are apprehensive or fearful). However, yesterday I approached this uncertainty with the weight of some powerful prayers behind me. I think sometimes I underestimate the power and strength that comes from my friendships in this time. I may be strong but it is only because of my friendships and my God (it's not me that's amazing).

I know I always underestimate the power of God in all of this. He has bigger, grander more magnificent plans than I can imagine and He will have the glory in this.

But in these times when I feel helpless, anxious and worrying I am blessed to have some amazingly strong people around me. My justgiving pages have shown me how incredible you all are to support our family like this. Life isn't always easy but it's worth celebrating because we only get one chance here on earth. From the bottom of my heart a huge thank you for the love, kindness, prayers, food and financial support. I am blown away by your love for others. **Thank you.** #togetherwearestrong

"On the very morning, I lit a candle for Laura. I prayed that Laura's light would be steady and strong. I know how courageous and brave she was fighting her illness and I believe that she will remain a shining light in all our lives."

"Yes we all have our fearful days, our days of being human. But it is important not to let that feeling take over or to sit alongside it and have tea with it
(And that is not an easy path or easy for me to say)."

– Laura Stephenson

"Life isn't always easy but it's worth celebrating because we only get one chance here on earth."

– Laura Stephenson

So today was exactly what I thought it was going to be and kind of hoped it wouldn't be. I saw my consultant and got some bad news. They think the swelling I have had recently under a lymph node could show that there has been a negative change in my circumstances. My blood cancer marker is also rising and is now above that from when I was diagnosed

On a day like today your head space is never where it should be and doing anything but just sitting still is never going to happen! Days like today I find hard. As anyone can imagine they must be; However, in these dark moments I am still being shown the joy and light in the days that I have.

♡ I bumped into a friend who even though going through her own mess made me smile and laugh and then I read this lady's post online.

He didn't STOP it... but I do believe He can & HAS used it for good. Not just for others but in my own heart too.

He's changed my heart. Opened my eyes. Showed me what MATTERS. Helped me see each day for the beauty that it is. & taught me more about deep-rooted JOY than I ever realized was possible.

At 29, yeah I'd rather go back to a "normal" life. But since I can't, and won't ever be able to even when the cancer is GONE...I'll let God use the rain to help me BLOOM through the storm.

The past 2 years have been an INTENSE discovery of God's love, of a deeper relationship with Him, & of ultimate trust when things just don't make sense and are downright terrifying. So terrifying that I can't even take another step.

But with Him I can. With Him I can enjoy days like this even with hard stuff right around the corner & cancer & chemo wreaking havoc on my body. Because He's already there in that next moment. He gives me courage. He makes me brave.

We may not see the full picture of WHY we go through what we go through, but we can fully TRUST that we can GROW through what we go through IF we understand that God works EVERYTHING together for the good of those who love Him. Even cancer.

So take THAT, stupid cancer. {insert middle finger here}

See ya soon, mr. CT machine. 🤳

Today has made me realise, my life is not in my consultants hands it is in God's hands. My body was made perfect and it will be perfect again. Have a good day.

When life chucks fear and negativity at you; what can you do?! In your own strength there is nothing you can do.

I struggled with that fear and negativity yesterday but once again have decided to look at that fear in the face and for what it is. It is an attack from the enemy in this battle that I am fighting. Since I have not been given a spirit of fear from God I must fight it off and not let myself stand in it. I know this battle has already been won by my God, healing is mine and it will happen for me. Some days I just wish it would happen soon. You do get a bit fed up of being the ill one; the girl constantly fighting for something brighter; the girl who needs to push to get the treatment that will give me the best chances.

Then I do a full reverse and remember that it is all in HIS timing and it's not a bad thing to wait because the amount of people I am meeting and the impact I am having sharing my faith is because His work is not done with this yet. Waiting in this isn't my idea of fun, and it is deeply frustrating at times but I don't want to miss out on this deeper level of faith that I know I have. It is exciting to see God in everything I do, to hear His voice and see His direction for my life. I love that I am totally dependent on His spirit to bring my healing; what a testimony it will be and how much glory in that miracle when I can say medically it is gone!

I was sent a few things from close friends yesterday and all of them were about fear. God loves to speak to me even in the midst of my storm, just to let me know He hasn't forgotten me and I need not be afraid. What a blessing to have a God that sends three or four people to tell you the same thing. It's never a coincidence!

Finally, I know that every day I get up and fight this thing that doesn't belong, is a day that I am one step closer to the doctors wondering where it went. It's also making the enemy terrified because if I can shout that I am a miracle because of the God I love what kind of impact will that have on people I meet?! So get running enemy because I am not letting the fear you give me pull me down and I will have my day shouting from the roof tops.

"She bounded over, full of energy and told me in a fearless way about the spread of the condition. But she followed that up with an assurance that she felt great, not ill at all. She had an absolute conviction that her life was in His care and that He is tenderly loving her. She was radiant."

"For most of us with cancer all we want is someone to fight with us and tell us that's what they are doing."

– Laura Stephenson

May 2nd 2019 WHAT TO SAY

Sometimes in this walk I hear or am told things that pile on the fear factor for me. People don't know what to say when you tell them the medical facts. I do understand that it's hard on others but I have decided that I need to start every conversation with people by explaining about my faith; about my God that has given healing freely and that I do not have fear. I do not intend to go anywhere early (never been early for anything!).

I guess what I want to say in this post is, those conversations aren't easy. But also for all of you who take on those conversations when you don't know what to say but want to say something - **thank you**! For most of us with cancer all we want is someone to fight with us and tell us that's what they are doing.

This is my promise and I stand on it because I know the power of my God. To all those people who stand beside me thank you; to all those who look at me and say 'You look so well' …………. thank you; to those that fight and pray with me, thank you. You are my constant source of positivity and I love you for it! For those that tilt their head to one side, and give me that 'I'm sorry' look; please don't be because you don't have any idea of the power of the God I serve. Your negativity to this situation isn't going to impact that power and it isn't helpful. It's never easy to know what to say (I understand that) but equally we all have one thing in common the desire to FIGHT #bemorekind

May 14th 2019 INTIMACY

Over the last few days God has been speaking to me about intimacy with Jesus, deliverance and breakthrough. I really want to share what I hope is an encouraging post this morning.

This battle I am in, has been the most draining, toughest and tested my mental capacity no end! It is the biggest one I will ever fight. But fight I will because it is going to be the battle that brings with it the biggest rainbow. I will be an old lady still singing my battle song for everyone to hear at 90 of that I am certain.

It is really easy in the midst of a battle for us to look all around at the devastation that is taking place and become disheartened. We hear voices of 'Will it ever end?'; 'Is it really possible?' Darkness has a great way of covering over the truth if we let it. We can look at something and it looks so different in the darkness.

Fear is that darkness in my situation right now. It comes into my mind often and wants to sit down and stay; It is hard to get rid of and I find myself entertaining those thoughts which pull me into worry or anxiety.

Today I have a scan. There is the capacity for that darkness to take over, for it to whisper in my ear "who do you think you are to be healed". In these moments I stand on what has been promised me in His word. I spin round and look that whisper in the eye and say, "Who am I not to be healed?"

As I went to bed last night I heard a shout and cry from Heidi's room. She sleeps really well and very deeply so it's always a surprise to hear a sound from her. I jumped out of bed and probably moved faster than I have in a while! Going into her room I found her sat up in bed, saying "but I want the other one". I have no idea what she was dreaming or referring too but I realised that her nightlight had gone out which is what had woken her. Heidi loves her nightlight and since being a baby needs that light to make her feel safe and secure when she sleeps. At five almost six she should probably be able to sleep without it but if it helps her I am happy to indulge it for as long as she needs me to.

In this moment I heard God so clearly say to me, "I am you light, I will not go out and I will light up your darkness so you need not be afraid". I had a little chuckle that He was using something so obvious to talk to me. But in that moment I realised I have no reason to fear, my breakthrough of light is coming. He is going to bring light into this darkest of situations. Simply because as our father in heaven that is what he does and longs to do for his children! I heard so many promises that are in His word in that moment and I realised that sometimes if we light up our fears then we have nothing to fear.

So as for today and my results day, you are nothing to fear. I have a light that promises to have more power in it than anything fear can throw at me. The end result for me is one of light, praise and glory to the God who heals and loves his children

Don't let fear sit with you. Don't let that darkness make you think that there is nothing good at the end of the battle and understand that when you put a light on only then can you see clearly that Hope is on your side.

May 20th 2019   HOW TO FIGHT THE BATTLE

Today is results day. Would love to say that even on these days I am filled with positivity, peace and understanding but that is not the case because I am human; and regardless of your faith or relationships we are created to feel fear and worry. But it is on these days that I realise just how big this mountain is that I need to move. Thankfully I don't have to do this on my own (now that would be terrifying!). I get to do this with my God right by my side, encouraging me in the word that this battle is one where victory is already secured. So this morning, encouraged by some good friends I have sat down with my trusty notebook and opened up God's word. Psalm 118:14-18 says everything I want to say today. •

As I read this passage a song played on my phone;
'This is how I fight my battles'.

Simply put, by staying in His word I fight my best fight. I don't need anything else, just the strength and promises of the God I serve. I will forever praise Him for my healing and give Him the glory! So everyone knows and gets sick of hearing it.

Over the weekend I had the opportunity to explain how I am fighting this battle to some lovely ladies. I love being able to tell people about God and sitting this morning I really feel that it is time to step it up a gear and do something that fills me with apprehension. I believe that it is now time for me to not only talk about my faith to people but to start praying for people who are sick or in need of some kind of healing. For many of you, you will know that this is not within my comfort zone.

98

I can tell you now there will be times I chicken out but if this is what I am asked to do, I should (in the words of a popular sports brand) –

"Just do it!"

I have no idea of the impact or reason behind it. But how exciting to be in a position to use this rubbish situation for His glory! Who knows what we will see happen, miracles are His handiwork!

May 22nd 2019   AT THE TOP OF ....

My results will be official tomorrow and barring my oncologist totally missing something on Monday, everything looks to be stable and not growing! This to me is great news and the power of my God.

Sometimes it is overwhelming being on this rollercoaster and I don't think it ever just applies to cancer. We all have situations we have had or are going through where our emotions, thoughts and paths feel like a rollercoaster. When we go down it feels like we will never get back up the other side.

It's like one of those old rollercoasters where there is a pulley system to get you back up to the top, it would grind and make awful noises. It would also feel like it was taking forever to pull the full weight of those carriages up that steep climb.

Have you ever felt like that climb is just too much? All you want to do is sit back and get to the top as fast as possible away from those thoughts and emotions that threaten to slide you back down.

Being in a path like that sucks. It's often not fair and we don't understand why. It is totally normal and human to feel like this but from one rollercoaster ticket holder to another don't let that steep climb put you off from sitting back in the seat of your rollercoaster and going up.

We may never understand why, but please know whether you have a faith like I do or you don't do faith, there is something beautiful at the top of that rollercoaster climb for everyone. You have the strength and you can make the choice to go up! It is a choice. So find those that love you, surround yourself with them, give them a seat on your rollercoaster and make the choice to climb. It isn't easy but it is **totally** worth it and rollercoaster rides don't last forever.

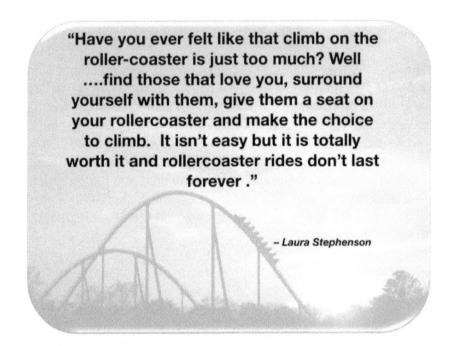

"Have you ever felt like that climb on the roller-coaster is just too much? Well ….find those that love you, surround yourself with them, give them a seat on your rollercoaster and make the choice to climb. It isn't easy but it is totally worth it and rollercoaster rides don't last forever ."

– Laura Stephenson

"Growing up with her was truly a blessing. She's been an inspiration; a true light in my life. I'll always treasure her and be thankful for her."

"Even as a child she had a fun and caring spirit that shone through."

"Our minds keep going back to our wonderful times in France. Laura was such a lovely girl. These memories will stay with us for ever."

"Laura has left our lives but has failed to leave our hearts."

A mixed bag so I finally have the exact measurements of each tumour in my currently imperfect body. A mixed bag could mean so many things, a mixed bag of opinions, a mixed bag of sports results or a mixed bag of sweets. It can mean different things to different people and ultimately depends on how you view it.

We have a choice on how we view things and boy is it easy to view them surrounded by troubles and doom, but if I am learning one thing it's that viewing it like that doesn't do us any favours. It brings our whole approach to this beautiful life down. It affects our mood, our food and how we spend time with others.

I know that the choice isn't an easy one. We listen to the whispers as ever that we aren't good enough. That this circumstance will never change and who are we to expect it too. I would love a mixed bag of sweet things right now; to be told 'we can't see anything there anymore' but I am learning. Perseverance in the midst of a storm is something pretty special to be taught.

What I love in all of this is the difference I see in myself and what I love even more is that my God never gives me a mixed bag. He is the same today, yesterday and will be the same tomorrow! His love for me doesn't change and the promises in His word will never change.

> ... .e, in the place of honor, right alongside God. (Hebrews 12:1~2 THE MESSAGE)
>
> • I am God's masterpiece—His handiwork, created in Christ Jesus to do the good things He prepared for me to do. I declare on this day that I will see the things that come my way as God's perfect plan to develop my character to match my calling. I will walk in His ways for me and give Him praise for the way He made me for the rest of my days.
>
> For we are God's handiwork, created in Christ Jesus to do good works, which God prepared in advance for us to do. (Ephesians 2:10)

My mixed bag is what the doctors perceive it as, that's their opinion. They are trained and wonderful people. But I see that mixed bag as something that can change and I know that's what my God intends to do for me!

I am reading the most amazing book at the moment. Here are pictures that are my prayers for this week. My body may not be perfect right now but it was created perfectly and I know that at the end of this rubbish situation He has a calling for me to follow for the next fifty years (at least) so I will take my mixed bag, mix it up and choose the next source of treatment knowing He has it hand and I can choose to enjoy this beautiful life I have been given with my best friend, my three gorgeous girls, amazing family and the most incredible friends. What's not to love about that?!

return to me with all their heart." (Jeremiah 24:7)

• I declare right now that I will not fear bad news or hard things that I may face. They do not have any control over my heart or my relationship with Jesus. Instead, I will cling to God's Truth, which never changes with the news I receive. Truth is what I will build the foundation of my life upon! Yes, my heart belongs to the Lord and I fully trust in Him, even when my feelings beg me to doubt His goodness. Feelings don't have the final say; Truth absolutely does.

They will have no fear of bad news;
their hearts are steadfast, trusting in the LORD.

(Psalm 112:7)

June 19th 2019   MAKE THE MOST OF EVERY DAY

So what's happening in my world at the moment... as ever it's a whole mixture of things from stresses at work, to fun with the girls! Life often brings highs and lows and in the middle of it all cancer really doesn't care if you are finding life easy or hard. On reflection I have decided to find that joy in the midst of it all, whilst understanding that you don't always have to be smiling.

At the moment I am on a break from chemo; not my choice, not sure whether it's a good thing or not and equally not quite sure what God has in mind for me at the moment. But what I do know is **He is good and loves me.**

Before I go into details I must say that I truly believe honesty is the best policy, and yet I can understand that for some people reading my honesty can be scary for them too. But in order to make a difference and hopefully inspire people to make the most of every day you have, I think honesty is absolutely the way it should be!

A little insight into the world you get thrust in to when you have cancer and your treatment stops. (Even for a month or two) It is terrifying! That fear of the unknown, of thinking every single second; Is it growing some more? Am I getting new symptoms to worry about?

I am not fighting back! It is very scary. It is constantly there and you feel like you have really lost control. The plan for me is to (prayers needed) get into the trial that is available with a new trial of immunotherapy drugs. Now would you believe if your tumour (like mine) grows on the left side then immunotherapy drugs seem to be the most effective for you! Thank you God!

This trial is in London so a trip down there every two weeks won't make life any simpler but it will mean I am stepping into tackling my situation.

However, at the moment my lungs are giving me a hard time, I can't have steroids to fix that as I would then not be allowed the trial treatment. So for now we are putting up with the lungs not behaving! I am taking more turmeric than I care to and probably will turn orange with the amount I take but if it brings the inflammation down in my lungs then that's a winning combo!

In all of this I have to look at the bigger picture. Why am I not on treatment at the moment? What is God's plan for all of this, and how can I continue to bring glory back to Him when I feel a little lost and distant?

What I have realised in this wasteland that is cancer, is I don't have to have all the answers, I don't have to control anything and patience is something that we should be proud to learn. That is so much easier said than done!

I am still listening in to Him because my promises come from God and they are unchanging. That is a huge comfort when you feel lost, because even though things are sent to knock me off course (a horrible working week or more symptoms of this horrible disease) I know that standing on what is written and focusing on learning those bible verses is the best thing right now.

When I am weak, or paralysed by fear, is when Gods strength really steps up a notch because at my lowest points He has promised to be my strength. My breakthrough is coming and the rainbow will show up for me soon of that I am sure...

I am waiting for that day when they look at my scan and can see nothing that concerns them and my body is fearfully and wonderfully made again! And you know what, when people throw unbelief at me, I simply look at them and think don't worry about me because I have a whole army behind me. I might some days struggle for positivity but my

Kenneth Copeland ● @Copelan... · 5h ∨
Resist the temptation to worry. When you engage in worry, you are really saying, "LORD, You can't handle this." You are saying that your problem is bigger than God. Resist the urge to fear, trust The LORD, and speak faith-filled words over the situation. #castyourcares #BVOV

Faith-filled words
dominate the law
of sin and death.

-Kenneth Copeland-

strength, because it is based on something supernatural, never waivers! I will beat this and all glory will be given to Him above!

Isaiah 43;18-19

"Laura has been an amazing Goddaughter and I have been immensely proud of her. She is our first and last thought every day."

"A little insight into the world you get thrust in to when you have cancer and your treatment stops. It is terrifying!

That fear of the unknown,
of thinking every single second,
Is it growing some more?
Am I getting new symptoms to worry about?
I am not fighting back !
It is very scary.
It is constantly there and you feel like you have really lost control."

—*Laura Stephenson*

"In these times when I feel helpless, anxious and worrying I am blessed to have some amazingly strong people around me.

....

– *Laura Stephenson*

"If you see God in your situation or not, or it's too dark to see anything, God moves even when you don't see it or feel it. He has not deserted you and He will pull you through."

— *Laura Stephenson*

June 26th 2019   I'M GOING TO DANCE!

Back again...

After five weeks off treatment (yes it's as scary as it sounds!) we are back at the hospital to hear the next lot of treatment plans. That is the not so scary bit. Because when you have a plan you can beat or fight anything! Cancer takes so much away from you, but one of the worst things is that it takes away any kind of control. Therefore, I am gaining back my land (that I am promised) and making a stand that I will not let it take any more control out of my hands or from God.

This meeting is just one of many but it will allow me to ask about more trials, understand the next treatment plan and again tell those in the NHS managing my care that my God is so much bigger than all of this. What's some harmless bragging!!!!!

I am excited to see what is to come, and still in it all trusting that all of this is only going to bring about a **breakthrough.**

I have been blessed so far and I will continue to be blessed in all of this. Last week I met a lovely guy who is really excited to help me start up a bowel cancer support group here in Preston. Our family are so precious and amazing at being supportive but I think it's so important to talk to those going through the same as you. Talking blesses, talking helps & talking is what I do best! It can be scary but sharing those fears or worries is a positive as no one should go through this alone!

I'll dance into this meeting because my body is going to (with His help) beat this invasion of naughty cells and when in doubt why not dance!

June 30th 2019   BEING PATIENT IS HARD

A new treatment! I am now on a drug form of chemotherapy which I take at home and don't have a pump fitted. The side effects are very similar to the drugs I have had before so not expecting anything drastic.

I am so thrilled to be in this position to have another lot of chemo.

The nay sayers putting me down with talk of 'well it is your third line' have no idea how blessed I am. I get to have a third line lot of chemo! God has me in the palm of his hand!

Saying that I really feel that I need to say, regardless of if you see God in your situation, or it's too dark to see anything, God moves even when you don't see it or feel it. He has not deserted you and He will pull you through. His heart for you is full of love, and he just wants to pour out blessings on your life. We don't always see it, if we are in the middle of a storm it's so easy to see black rain clouds and forget that **rain** brings new life. Keep looking upwards, keep expecting miracles and even when you don't feel like it, look for blessings because **you** are more than worth it and more!

This topic of **rain and breakthrough**, bringing miracles and washing over me is so important and really speaks to me at the moment. I don't know how God will do it, but He will make my body whole again, He will restore and an immovable impossible situation is nothing to Him.

Today I read this post by a great guy, Nate Johnston & then a friend just confirmed how relevant it was for me by sending it to me. If I'm honest, recently I have struggled to make time for God and have felt a bit distant. Some days it's hard to battle constantly, day in day out putting your heart and soul into a fight; looking upwards and letting Him lift you up or shelter under His wings. I think with me it probably has a lot to do with control. I like to be in charge and have a clear plan of what is going to happen When I don't have that I find the road a little tough to follow.

This week I dare you to pray dangerous, life-changing prayers. Ask for heaven to come interrupt every facet of your life. Ask for encounters that ruin you for the mundane and ordinary. Ask for signs, wonders, and supernatural kisses from God daily that cause you to see through the lens of the realm you have access to. Ask for MIRACLES and such potent displays of POWER that pull you out of settling for cheap talk and inspiration. Ask for the rain in dry places of your heart and life and watch it come. Ask for fresh RIVERS to flow out of the inside of you. Ask to DREAM again, but dreams that challenge you and pull you into your destiny. Ask for the nations, because they are already yours! Call down FIRE upon the altar of your home and see legacy change. Speak BREAKTHROUGH over immovable and impossible situations. Prophesy RESTORATION, recompense, and restitution. Command sickness to leave, affliction to cease, and bodies and minds to be whole. Pray when you don't feel like it, when it's a sacrifice, when it's a worship in the middle of the storm and watch as God FLIPS THE SCRIPT on every powerless circumstance you lay your eyes upon. Your story of woe is turning into your testimony of WOAH that is going to UNLOCK the prison doors and set people, families, and regions free. God is going to use your mouth to CREATE and bring forth life in the days to come and the results will shock you. So I dare you ..

Again I think I am subtly being taught to be patient and to trust that I can't and shouldn't have control and sometimes it's about just sitting and being silent. I don't have to pray but I do need to just sit with Him.

Have a good week everyone, prayers for my lungs and the inflammation to go down would be amazing if you pray!

July 2nd 2019   GIANTS CAN BE DEFEATED

I don't think I post enough in honesty. It's very easy to have a positive face on to the outside world but it's a lot harder to say "today has been a bit hard, I read... or I have had thoughts of..." Apart from bringing it all to God in prayer who do you tell, who do you cry on or shout with that, "It's not supposed to be this way" But today has been a bad thought day. It's not been a negative day, quite the opposite but it has been a bit knocking my positivity day.

Reading this tonight has made me realise we all feel like this. It's normal to not always feel happy or positive particularly when you have a huge giant constantly over your thoughts or behind you. Other people's words can be such a blessing and we should take time to read or listen, as well as taking on board what is out there for us. God sends what we need just when we need it. Thank you for this Lord, I am blessed!

I had a vision and I saw Jesus come alongside these daughters of God that were so tired of fighting this giant throwing the stones of the Word of God at it and I saw Jesus lean in close and whisper in their ear. "JUST ONE MORE SHOT" He helped lift their weary arm and as they went to throw the stone I saw what looked like a HUGE waterfall of water and fire come crashing down upon them and I KNEW it was the revelation of His love, the refreshing of His Spirit and the washing of the Word. As they threw the final stone I saw their hearts BURSTING forth with new life, healing and wholeness. Life came back to their eyes and faces and the stone hit the giant between the eyes and down he went and a HUGE mantle of peace fell upon the daughters of God, the peace that is promised in Christ was manifesting in their lives in new and fresh ways.

Daughters of God, if you have been battling the 'giant' of anxiety, it's coming down in Jesus name. It's not bigger than Jesus, it just wants to look like it is. God has heard your cries, He has heard your prayers. Don't give up, throw the stone of faith again, because the tipping point of your healing, deliverance and breakthrough is UPON YOU.

This was written for me today. I am strong even when I feel weak. it may look like a giant but giants can be defeated. Just one more stone will see healing released and the Giant falling.

110

"We all need to be a bit more vocal with our positivity. Stepping outside of our comfort zones to let someone know we are thinking of them, or how they have had a positive effect on us or even better to let them know we are praying for them."

–Laura Stephenson

"This week I am going to challenge myself to speak to those people I don't know. ....
It's very easy to get distracted by life, and to slip into the comfort of who we know and what we know...........

Imagine if that lady hadn't spoken to me this morning?

I can honestly say my day wouldn't have been as brightened as it was!

– Laura Stephenson

Sometimes in life we feel that we have so much thrown at us, and that it is more than we can handle. On our own strength, yes it probably is more than we can handle mentally and physically. It could overwhelm us completely!

But I'll let you into a little secret; with God on our side it is never more than we can handle! In everything, I am slowly (takes me a while!) figuring out that I must keep, in his strength, through Him and with Him in me, in order to figure out how to navigate this path. Nothing will be achieved in my own strength! We must not take for granted that we have enormous capabilities if we rely and become dependent on him.

I remember with one of my college friends we used to say God may take you to an edge but He will never let you fall!

Recently I have felt that I have been pushed to that edge. Treatment is ok. I know God has my healing in hand but work has been tough! I'm feeling a little bit worn down by circumstances and that has meant I have felt further from Gods strength than normal. But I have decided no more! I will not let fear derail me. I won't let it stop me from finding joy, and negativity around me can find somewhere else to rest its head!

I have been asking God to speak to me. I find being distant from Him (my own fault) creates a really unsure feeling inside of me. Today He once again came through for me. As I dropped Heidi and a friend off at holiday club this morning a lady that has read my posts on here told me that I am an inspiration! I never find it easy to get compliments from people, I'm never quite sure what to say in response. None of this is me, it's all down to Him. But at a time when I am needing that boost someone stops me to tell me how I have impacted them, and that is just what the doctor ordered. It also got me thinking, we all need to be a bit more vocal with our positivity. Stepping outside of our comfort zones to let someone know we are thinking of them, or how they have had a positive effect on us or even better to let them know we are praying for them.

This week I am going to challenge myself to speak to those people I don't know, by listening to the prompting of God.

It's very easy to get distracted by life, and to slip into the comfort of who we know and what we know. But imagine if that lady hadn't spoken to me this morning?! I can honestly say my day wouldn't have been as brightened as it was in that moment. So to the lady who stepped out to speak to me - Thank You!

Back at the hospital today for my chemo tablets, waiting in bloods to say if I can have them yet! Get praying people that my bloods are ok, I can get cracking again and that my lungs and lymph nodes respond to the new treatment!

July 29th 2019   TESTING OR NOT

Listening to a very dear friend preach in church this morning and I won't steal her preach but it has helped remind me that the tests we go through are not for God to test us. He knows how big our faith is (even when we aren't sure how big it is!). He sees the troubles, joy and faith in our hearts and souls. When we are in a test it is for **us** to understand how big, deep and wide our faith is!

I spend quite a bit of time within Heidi's school environment chatting to her friends' parents. Many of these have now become my friends. Some of the mums I chat to have a faith like mine, however at the same time it is quite different to mine. They believe that God tests us to see how big our faith is. Whilst I love talking to them about their faith, I equally love that mine is different. You see my God doesn't test me, He hasn't given me cancer because He is a loving, compassionate father. He is however loving that my faith is deeper, and I am more dependent on Him than ever before because of this rubbish situation.

Don't ever think God has forgotten you, or that He has given you hard things or storms in your life, or that He leaves during those storms. It is in those moments He wants you to trust him; so allow it, choose to have a faith, choose for it to be deep and dependent on God. As we head into the summer, school holidays and making memories, let's remember to stop and refresh. If we want to see just how big our faith is, sometimes we have to stop in the midst of our own created busy lives. • Remember God is a good God and He wants us to have a faith where we trust in Him completely. But we can't do that if we put off spending time with Him.

113

I am so excited to head off on holiday for my sister's wedding! I do however need prayer for tomorrow that my bloods come back right so I can start the next lot of chemo. If you do pray, please pray for this and that my lungs start to improve.

July 30th 2019 A COINCIDENCE

Just a very quick update. My bloods came back up so I am back on the chemo! Celebrations all round. They rose from 0.78 to over 3.5! Now it could be a coincidence, but for them to rise that much makes me think it's more likely to be all those prayers sent up!

If I can be cheeky again, please can you pray for the pain I am having in my side. It is starting to really stop me doing things with the girls and I hate that! Plus, I want to enjoy my holiday with my family not be trying to sit still to get rid of it! Thank you everyone.

August 8th 2019   SMALL BLESSINGS

Last night I had a bath. Now that sounds like a normal thing for most of us but for me it hasn't been. I have had baths but with a constant fear of my PICC line getting wet.

Last night marked a huge point for me in this battle. When things seem against you (which is how I have felt over the last month or so) God gives me that nudge which shows me this isn't forever. It is a battle I can win and I am not alone in this.

I read a passage this week by Lana Vawser, and it really lined up with lots of things happening in my life at the moment •

She talked about being confident. If anything recently I have felt as far away from confident as ever; reading her word made me remember that I am blessed because I can have **confidence** in his word. I have been pulled from one negative comment to another; allowing the ground on which I stand to feel like sinking sand but the ground on which I stand is built on my faith, and on truth. It is firm, but just how firm I find it depends a lot on my relationship with God. What does it mean for me? How much I am putting into my prayer life? Am I delighting in all He brings to my life?

In particular, in this word, I read with a smile on my lips about faith muscles. Now most of you know that as I set off on my holidays for my sister's wedding I had a pain in my right side. It honestly felt like a knife was stabbing me with every breathe or action. I am hoping that this was due to a pulled muscle. (I feel a lot better now!)

So imagine my surprise when this one word talked about spiritual faith muscles that God is building in His daughters. It is painful but He is building these within us to push back the enemy and to move us forward. Maybe the pain I had was for a greater reason; maybe to stand firm on his word we have to go through some troubles because that's when our feet become rooted. Constantly in His word we are reminded to not let our world fears or doubts disarm us. He promises us more and He promises us healing.

Don't let the world disarm or bring about fears that aren't in line with what the bible says and appreciate all those small blessings (like having a bath) we find along the way! We are blessed beyond anything we ever thought possible already!

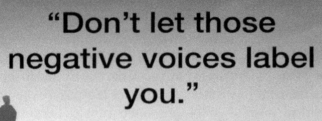

"Don't let those negative voices label you."

– *Laura Stephenson*

Laura was a beacon of light. God was her inspiration.

What an amazing person! A demonstration of Christ, Love and Hope. Laura has touched my own life so much. Her incredible faith and positivity were contagious. I pray I can be more like her.

Today I read an article posted by a fellow twin mummy. She had posted an article by a lady called Katy in America. I decided to read it and then read the blurb at the bottom that explained who Katy is. After reading about her lovely husband and two boys it said 'I am a stage 4 cancer survivor'

Yesterday I led next to Mark before bed and told him that I had been having negative thoughts a lot in the last day or so.

As if by 'magic' I then read a blog by a lady who had been given that label of stage four just like me. She like me, clearly said 'no thanks' to that label and went on to show them she wouldn't be a statistic!

If I believed in magic, I'd think this was all some lovely coincidence just when I needed it most.

Good job that's not what I believe because otherwise I would be basing my future on something that could equally change in a puff of smoke. Instead I am basing it on feelings and experience. You can't argue with those! They are the truth for me.

This article got me thinking though.

Labels suck most of the time. Who are we to be another statistic?! Let's not be defined by labels!

I wasn't created in a factory where everyone got the same bodies; where we all acted the same or had the same personality.

No I was created wonderfully, and uniquely. Therefore, how can I now be defined and told what my body will do by other humans because we are following a textbook or going off others' experiences.

My body was created perfectly and it will be perfect (or at least cancer free) one of these days... because my faith tells me that I am not defined by labels, or others and I can believe in more. God created me!

117

So the next time I hear a negative voice telling me otherwise I am going to raise up my voice and with the truths I have been given I am going to tell those voices where to go (in a very polite way of course!)

Don't let those negative voices label you.

You are not like anyone else; you were created perfectly; you are perfect in Gods eyes.

When circumstances make you feel like you are anything less than perfect, or our eyes try to get us to believe the mess around us is how it has to be. Don't trust it. It's never about what our eyes see in the physical; it's about what we have faith in.

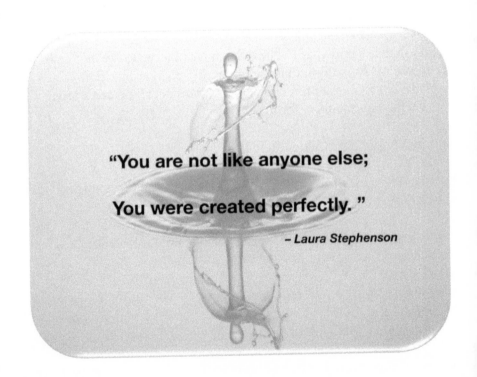

"You are not like anyone else;

You were created perfectly."

– Laura Stephenson

I know this blog is to tell you about my treatment and where I am up to but I wanted to take this post to tell you about my fantastic family and my wonderful husband.

I would be lost without my family recently and my sister's wedding has shown me just how much extended (adopted friends into family) family I have supporting and loving me! It absolutely blows my mind to see that amount of love coming my way! So a huge thank you to you all!

Now it is the eve of my wedding anniversary tonight We will have been married eight years tomorrow and I love my husband more today than I ever have,

I am pretty sure when people get married and say those vows they never imagine for one minute that they will be tested. Eight years ago I stood next to a man and we promised to love each other through everything. Eight years later and that is exactly what we are doing! And we are fighting it pretty well together!

We never imagined this many hospital visits, the scan anxiety, the mountain we have to climb or the change in appearances we have to deal with. But I love looking at our relationship now to where we were 8 years ago and seeing the changes because we are so much stronger not only in our faiths but in this together.

I have so much support, love, kindness and positivity from my husband that I really would be lost without it. When I am having a wobble he reminds me of the promises that God has given us. He reminds me just how strong I am and how we can move mountains because of our faith Every once in a while it is so important to tell those we love just how amazing their support to us is!

Who have you got that needs to hear how they boost you? Give an extra thanks this week to someone that lifts you up!

#dontgiveup #alwayskeepfighting #stupidcancer

#itdoesntstandachance

119

"I choose to enjoy this beautiful life
I have been given, with my best friend, my
three gorgeous girls, amazing family and the
most incredible friends.
What's not to love about that?"

– Laura Stephenson

"Every once in a while it is so
important to tell those we love
just how amazing their support is.
Who have you got that needs to
hear how they boost you up?"

– Laura Stephenson

I wanted to post tonight because I have felt like God has been talking to me all day. So often in this battle I go through each day feeling like I am so distant from my faith and then I have a day where He just draws me back in and reminds me of all of his promises and who He is!

Today I shared with a friend a feeling that God had placed on my heart. He knew her situation and He asked me to share something with her. In doing so I reminded myself that I must not be in a hurry to escape a situation.

Now please hear me right when I say this. I am not enjoying this battle, I had no desire to place my body or mind under such stress or to put so much rubbish (chemo) into my body. However, I think we rush through life sometimes wanting to get to the next stage. Yes, I would love to be cancer free, like I say I am not enjoying the cancer battle (it sucks!) but in the battle I have found a closeness to God and a deeper level of faith than I ever thought possible; plus, new friendships that I would not have had outside of this world!

That deeper level of faith has encouraged me to explore different areas of my faith that I have always just taken for granted. I know that is not something we should admit as Christians. For me Communion has always played a huge part in my faith, I just think I never fully understood the connection it has to healing.

I have read and keep coming back to the verse in Isaiah 53: 4-5 'by His stripes we are healed'

I know that even some Christians view healing in very different ways, and I am sure some don't want me to get my hopes up. However, why can't healing be ours today if it says it is ours. I am not naive enough to believe that what I have isn't huge but equally if we speak out the words promised to us, read our bibles, take communion and speak over our bodies then we clearly understand and can't deny the power of the cross.

121

Finally, I have had the same thing said to me, three times today just in different ways. When God speaks to you like that you really can't deny what he is trying to get rooted in to your spirit and soul. Thank you to my friends who have an ear open to Him and are happy to share what is on their hearts!

Let people know you are praying for them. Tell them what is on your heart and always be prepared to just sit before you run to the next step

September 4th 2019   I'M JUST ME

Short post I hope...

Sat at Rosemere waiting for the results of my bloods. I really struggle sometimes when people say how amazing I am or what an inspiration I am, to know what to say back to them. I am simply me just doing what anyone would do in this situation. No it isn't always easy; and it comes with sacrifices as well as fear but as I have sat in the Rosemere waiting area this morning I have realised just how many of God's blessings I have been given in this battle!

I get to sit and read; no nausea; able to walk, and with no pain anywhere in my body.

A lady came in on a stretcher, and couldn't move. She just led asleep and yet she still had to go for radiotherapy! How horrible for her. There are a number of elderly waiting for hospital transport to get them home after a gruelling treatment. I have got to pray for all of them, prayers of strength, prayers of courage and prayers of healing.

I get to sit learning more about my faith and able to drive myself home once I am done. I can't complain about waiting or even having to be here. I am blessed!!

"Hope at times of chaos isn't easy but it is the best way to face your future, from a seat of joy, which must sound crazy when the mountain is so high and your body isn't behaving as it should, but facing it with joy makes me realise that I can have hope..."

– *Laura Stephenson*

"Enjoy the air in your lungs, drink in the beauty around you and take ten minutes out of a day to just sit, loving your own company."

–*Laura Stephenson*

Laura always managed to make everyone around her feel better. She always had wise words of support despite what she was personally dealing with. She will forever be the prime example of a super mummy, wife, daughter, sister and friend.

"The unwavering faith 'till the last. The joy on her face in the midst of suffering."

"Laura was a beautiful person in so many ways. She was a ray of light and happiness to everyone who knew her."

Ever onwards and as I head into today I know that God has me tucked under His wings. I don't know why this is the verse He keeps giving me but He knew the path before me four years ago when He first prompted this verse in my heart and then four years later this is how I try to walk every day. Hope, at times of chaos, isn't easy but it is the best way to face your future particularly from a seat of joy, which must sound crazy when the mountain before you looks so high and your body isn't behaving as it

should. For me facing this with joy makes me realise that I can have hope as this is not what was intended for my body! It was intended with **no** cancer.

Affliction isn't from God, but it does develop our faith beyond what we could ever have imagined plus it develops our patience! I never wanted this to last longer than a year but it has, so therefore I will dig deep and explore all of the things and promises that I can with my amazing faith. What a privilege to do that in the middle of a storm!

I always viewed prayer as something I had to do and think I misunderstood the power behind it. When you have hundreds of people standing with you in prayer it is an incredible feeling. It is faith in action and it is beautiful because we aren't arguing about what our God looks like. We are just connected. The power of prayer speaks to my body to line up with the word of God, faithful in prayer means that we don't stop doing that until my body is clear of cancer and meets everything it promises me in the bible. It can bring about miracles. What a way to live! #standinginhispromises #godisgood #romans12

So today hasn't been the day I hoped for. Lots of facts but not a lot of truth. I appreciate that doctors see things one way, and I think today just felt like another hit from a horrible disease. It has left me feeling quite rubbish and full of fear. I will need some time to pick myself up, dust off those facts and find the truth that I know is for me. When I feel like I can share I will. Prayers for my

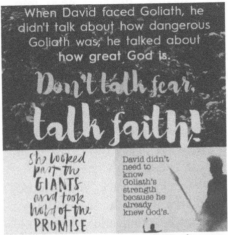

body to start lining up with the perfect way it ws created. To be would be amazing. We need to start seeing a different picture and one that I know is promised to me. I am going to sleep tonight to believe and trust in more than I can see around me. And believing that Goliath will fall and for David it only took one small stone because he had the power of God on his side !

September 27th 2019   IN THE MIDST OF THE BATTLE

Lots of things happening at the moment...

First an update for those of you who I haven't seen to speak too. My chemo is no longer working for me and it has now spread to my ovaries, with my lungs getting worse and a new growth on my liver. Obviously this wasn't the news I wanted but I am still here, being a mummy, wife, sister, daughter and friend so I am not going to panic just yet.. If I had put all my trust in man then yes I would be panicking big time, but I have a trust in a much stronger and higher power. Even in the face of bad facts that doctors give me, I still maintain that my God will be the one who reverses all of this and uses evil for good! Just wait and see!!

So we are still in the midst of the battle, and it's been an amazing week as God has really spoken to me about 'battles'. On Sunday a visiting pastor told me that Psalm 118; 8 was a great verse for me at the moment. "It is better to take refuge in the Lord than to trust in people."

Then I finally listened to a service on a blog sent by another member of my church family. The service was all about the battle not being mine to fight but it being God's battle and He will fight it for me.

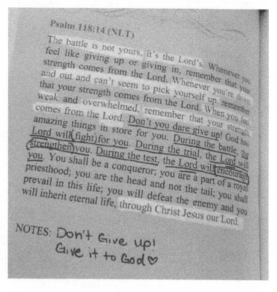

Just to cement all of this, I heard from a close family friend this morning (she clearly has her ears open to God) as she sent me this verse: Psalm 118; 14. Alongside it was a study that her cousin had been reading. The study started by saying 'the battle is not yours, it is the Lord's.'

It's in moments like this that I think God is really trying to get me to lie down on the promises of the bible and take full comfort that He has this covered. He has not left me. He has not given up. He will not fail me and He will HEAL me!

Don't ever think that God has forgotten you, despite what we sometimes see with our eyes or hear from those who have facts. He has everything in hand and loves us so completely that we will see His power in situations that we thought were end of the line situations!

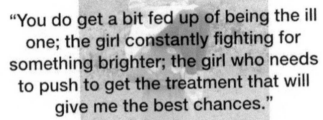

"You do get a bit fed up of being the ill one; the girl constantly fighting for something brighter; the girl who needs to push to get the treatment that will give me the best chances."

–Laura Stephenson

Laura was a beautiful person, inside and out. Her enthusiasm and cheerfulness were infectious. She had a wonderful faith which she wasn't afraid to share with people she met.

And sometimes I think that's enough now. Sorry this post may be a bit of a whinge but every now and then I reach that stage where I think; *"this is not what I signed up for"*. I am blessed and that I am more than aware of, but I would like a day where I am not fearful, I am not fighting and something seems to go my way.

I really hate cancer. It has the ability to rob you of your joy; to make you question if you can manage simple life situations you normally take for granted and to make you fear that you won't get to do all you have planned. It takes away your joy because you spend every situation wondering if this is as good as it gets or if others are thinking all doom and gloom around you but not voicing it. Little stresses seem magnified as you feel you are already on a battle ground but the arrows just keep flying at you! I am so annoyed and cross that it does this to me! It makes me look at the body which I believe was created perfectly, with annoyance and disgust! What right does it have to inflict these feelings, emotions and level of control over anyone!?!

So cancer I am ready for you to do one now. You don't belong! And you certainly have no authority over me! Sometimes we need to speak out against these things that we feel have control over our lives. We need to say **no more**! We look straight into the storm and we say, 'I will not be afraid anymore'. For too long you have taken my hope, my future and my happiness; and that level of control stops now!

I pray that over the coming weeks, for those of you that feel like this (it doesn't have to be cancer!) that you would feel the shift taking place where you move from a place of fear to a place of battle and then to a place of rest. That you see things through different eyes, and have a peace in your spirit that someone else has got this covered on your behalf! Don't give up, don't settle for that feeling of helplessness and don't believe the lies that this is as good as it gets!.

The last few weeks haven't been easy. I am waiting for bloods and tissue results that show mutations in them, the more mutations the more likely they are to have a trial for me.

Treatment has been stopped for now, because if I have treatment I then can't go into a trial but equally living in this limbo isn't the easiest place to be as it is here that you listen to those voices of negativity. You question the path you are taking and you feel as if you have stopped fighting the battle before you. It is in this place that I think God meets you full on, holds out his hands and asks you to step forward holding his hands because let's face it, this battle is one that I cannot fight on my own!

On a Sunday afternoon I have ended up sat with all three of my girls watching Frozen. Now my youngest girls have never watched this Disney movie before, and to watch their faces just captivated by the film has been such a joy! However, it has really spoken to me as well about the situation I am in. Now my close friend Meliza would definitely agree with me on this! Her take on Rapunzel was amazing!

Elsa in Frozen lives in this impossible situation, if she unleashes the power inside of her she fears that it will be too much. And yet there is someone in her camp that will stop at nothing to bring her sister home and right everything that is wrong.

Imagine that kind of love, that kind of loyalty and that kind of power. It isn't Anna's (Elsa's sister) battle to fight and yet she loves her sister so much that she can't just stand by and do nothing. There is the negativity that comes from Prince Hans, who is just out for himself. He whispers in the ears of anyone who will listen; lies, destruction and negativity. And wow it is so easy to listen to that when it is in your ear most days! No matter how much you try to block it out, or lock yourself in an ice tower, you can't get away from what the world tells you. You won't win this battle, there is nothing left for you, and you should just give up because hope is lost.

But is hope really ever lost? I don't think so. I have been reminded again and again this week to **rise up** and not give up! This is a big battle, and it is bigger than me, and maybe it is God's battle to fight not mine. In Frozen Elsa doesn't fight this battle, Anna does it on her behalf and gets hurt in the process. God sent his son to die for me on the cross to bring full healing and health to all that follow him. That must have been beyond painful to see that happen but He did it anyway. Ok so Frozen is a movie, but what if we can learn something from it?

It takes the kiss of true love to save the two sisters in Frozen, and I know that I have a God who truly loves me even more than that. He sent his son to die for me on the cross, and His power can transform any situation (Romans' 8;37). So I am loved, God is beyond loyal where his children are concerned and this is His battle to fight so I must just give it all over to Him and **trust**!

I don't see anything but a happy ending at the end of this tale....

November 3rd 2019 ALL THE BEST THINGS COME IN THREES

What do you say when your daughter says "Mummy will you be better soon? You have been poorly for such a long time now"

What do you do when you have had a week knowing that this is the path God has placed you on. It's been positive and then you get hit by a curveball!

What do you do when all you want to do is give up or go back to a time when life was so much simpler. When you had beautiful long hair that you **so** took for granted and you didn't mind looking in a mirror at the body God had given you. You have a good old cry! One of those really ugly ones, where you know if you looked in a mirror you would terrify the biggest monster! Because sometimes it's ok to not be ok and to let it out! Sometimes that's just what God wants us to do.

To fall before Him and say enough is enough. I can't do this anymore. This road is just too tough! God doesn't look at us in those moments and think,

'Wow she's an ugly crier!'

or

'What's she moaning about now?'

No, it's in those moments when He pulls you closer. He gets how hard it is. Trust me, he gets it! And in those moments he holds you closer than ever, because to Him you are more precious than you can imagine!

"Because sometimes it's ok to not be ok and to let it out!"

–Laura Stephenson

Last week I spent the week in Aberdeen. Due to not having any more treatment options open to me on the NHS I decided to look elsewhere and with the help of my family found a lot of information about Mistletoe therapy. Mistletoe therapy is used to encourage your own immune system to go into overdrive and fight off the cancer. I have to have a fever induced therapy in an IV plus an injection. It went well last week and the doctor was very pleased with my initial reaction. With this being said I have to go back in a week's time for another fever induced therapy. (Not keen on leaving my girls for yet another week!) so a few things to let you all know about. A few weeks before I booked the therapy God blesses me with some funding to pay for this therapy.

In all of this I have been desperate to hear God talking to me and I really feel like God has been talking about things happening in threes. I am not entirely sure what He has in mind and am waiting for it to be revealed to me. I hadn't realised, and had been told, that I would have two lots of fever inducing therapy across two weeks. However, on Friday the doctor told me that it would be three. I've had one and would go back for another two. One of my friends recently encouraged me to listen to some testimonies of God healing cancer. The guy that I love listening too, heard from God three times before he received healing. Finally, another friend sent me a few passages from the Bible, 1 kings :17. It is a story about a lady who obeys God by helping Elijah, when her son dies. She asks Elijah why God would allow this to happen. Elijah goes to the son

"And he stretched himself out over the child three times and cried out to the Lord, "O Lord my God, please let this child's life return to him. 1 Kings 17:21

He does it three times! And when Heidi asked me tonight when I was going to get better I said we wait on Gods healing. I asked her what she had learnt in Sunday school today, she told me the story above and said Elijah asked God three times to heal her son.

If we trust in Him, and are obedient to Him then He will bless us and give us more than we could possibly imagine. It's not easy! But boy is it worth it! Have a great week and be blessed indeed.

I ran the Preston half marathon and bumped into Laura at the start. I then ran ahead and towards the end, when I was struggling, I heard an encouraging shout from the other side of the road. Laura had spotted me and somehow knew my name...... Always encouragement.

"Maybe we just need to slow down.

Now don't start with the, 'but I don't have time to slow down' or 'I just have so much to get done today' excuses.

Because actually, will the world stop if you don't do that load of laundry or will everything really fall apart if you don't just nip to that place?"

No probably not !

– Laura Stephenson

I know I only shared a post last night but this morning sat over a green tea watching the world go by, I have been struck by another thought I wanted to share.

Maybe we just need to slow down.

Now don't start with the, 'but I don't have time to slow down' or I just have so much to get done today' excuses. Because actually will the world stop if you don't do that load of laundry or will everything really fall apart if you don't just nip to that place? No probably not!

At the moment I really do not have the strength in my lungs to get anywhere fast. Now I don't think God gave me cancer in my lungs, but the situation being what it is I have been forced to slow down! At the moment, gone are the days when I race to keep up with those who like to stride out, gone are my running days or rushing to get places on time. (Not that that ever happened before now anyway!) so I will settle for that slow steady stroll that I am forced to do.

In all of that though, it means that I truly appreciate what's happening around me, I stop to take everything in and all the little moments I missed, I get to see now because I am forced to just slow down and truly not take for granted the little things I see.

Two things I want to leave you with for the week. Is it time to slow down a little? I don't mean stop doing the normal household chores you have to get done but maybe take ten minutes out to just sit and have a cup of tea and watch the world go by outside. Life will still be there, busy and chaotic after your ten minutes. But it may smell a little sweeter than it did.

Also don't take for granted your wonderful body! What I would give at the moment to feel the normal rise and fall of my lungs! I didn't get to choose what happened to them, but if you can, choose to respect the body that has been given you. It is an incredible creation, it does just what you need it too when you need it.

135

So don't mess it up by wanting it to be any different or putting stuff into it that might ruin its wonderful mechanisms! Enjoy the air in your lungs, drink in the beauty around you and take ten minutes out a day to just sit loving your own company!

You are amazing!

November 19th 2019   IF IM BEING HONEST ITS BEEN TOUGH

When someone asks, "How are you?" as British people we tend to nod, smile and say, "Yeah not bad thanks".

But what about those times when that isn't how we feel. When your body is screaming give up; your lungs just can't get the air in they need and all you want to do is curl up and say see you later world!

I am not one for living in a place of feeling rubbish, where it's dark and everything is a bit sucky. But these last few weeks that's where I have been. I have cried, shouted and told God just what I think of this messed up situation. I am ready for healing, I am ready for my promises to be manifested and to say goodbye cancer!

But today has been a real turning point for me in my mind. Because God placed two worship songs on my heart.

I know I have some big battles coming up. For example, my time of the month seems to be giving me some horrendous problems with ovary pain that is honestly off the chart, leaving me unable to breathe and rolling around in pain. So we need to figure that out before the next one. My lungs are so full of things they shouldn't be that breathing is becoming scary and very difficult.

Prayer for those would be incredible!!

Today my family said goodbye and celebrated the life of an amazing lady; Mark's Grandma, Ennis Hargreaves.

Listening to how she came to know the Lord. How she led her family to know him; all the young people she taught about Him and how every step she took demonstrated her love for her saviour stopped me in my tracks a little. What an example she set! A true inspiration! We sang two songs chosen by her, the first was The Lord's my Shephard (psalm 23) and Because He Lives.

In Because He Lives a few lyrics struck me, I have attached a photo, of these lyrics but 'life is worth the living just because He lives.'

Because He lives I can face tomorrow

Because He lives all fear is gone

Because I know He holds the future

And life is worth the living

Just because He lives

Yes, it's tough, and I haven't felt much like it's worth it but actually I can face anything because I know that Jesus lives and because of that healing, forgiveness and love. It's a pretty incredible life to live!

"I am not one for living in a place of feeling rubbish, where everything is dark and sucky I have cried, shouted and told God just what I think of this messed up situation.

I am ready for healing and to say goodbye to cancer ! "

– Laura Stephenson

Finally, I sometimes forget that in all of this I sometimes need to lie down in green pastures and just surrender. Stop trying to figure it out or understand His time or plans. But mainly these lyrics say it all for me at the moment:

"I will trust in you alone.
And though I walk the darkest path,
I will not fear the evil one,
For You are with me, and Your rod and staff
Are the comfort I need to know."

I must TRUST. It sounds like such a simple concept but in any relationship this is one of the keys that binds people together. It's not easy to trust or have faith when the world screams something different at you, or you see, feel a certain way. Trust is so easily broken. But God has never let me down, He has never broken that trust. I'm pretty sure I have for him but he is the same today, yesterday and forever so he never will!

If God has said he will do something (Isaiah 58:8) then He will!

If there is a mountain in front of you, if your body or mind are screaming world truths at you and if it feels like it's never going to end.

I have something to tell you. It isn't easy but please **trust.** He has your back, He will pull you through and you will see that mountain conquered.

Just don't give up!

And if you need to sit in that place of 'it sucks', that's ok just don't make yourself comfy there because there is more for you!

"From the bottom of my heart a huge thank you for the love, kindness, prayers, and all your unswerving support. I am blown away by your love for me. "

– *Laura Stephenson*

Readings from the Celebration of Laura's Life
January 10th 2020

Julia Barnes – Mum

Laura was always a happy little girl who really enjoyed the company of others. She loved school and always had a very caring nature, especially with anyone younger than herself. Laura loved being a big sister to Emily and Harriet and would go any lengths to be there for them, whenever and wherever!

She was definitely a second mum to Harriet being 7 years older when she came along.

She was always very willing to participate in any sort of performing role; be it dancing, singing, playing a musical instrument – now who does that sound like?

Laura has always been very sociable. She struggled a bit when we moved to Lancashire from Essex, where she had known exactly where she fitted in, but soon found her feet, forming friendships at school and church and amongst our friends.

Once at Longridge High School and then Runshaw College she moved on in her church life independently from us and became baptised at Longton Church, the same group of people who have set up Crossgates church, where we are now. She formed many lasting friendships here and grew in her Christian life.

Although appearing confident Laura hated leaving home and cried when we dropped her off at Lincoln University. However, she stayed the course, meeting some special friends along the way.

She also phoned home on a trip away to friends in America, crying that she was missing us all so much............ but was enjoying it at the same time.

After University Laura worked for The Message Tribe and eventually met Mark which was a union so very blessed as they worked so well together as a team.

Laura loved her work as a fundraiser as she was out and about meeting volunteers, raising funds and forming self-help groups and generally being with people. She worked at Rosemere Cancer Foundation which supports cancer treatment throughout Lancashire and South Cumbria. She set up many fundraising schemes that have become annual events. From here, she worked for a technology company GB3, and then Cancer Help, a small local charity supporting those with cancer.

And in November 2019 she started a new fund-raising post with Heartbeat, a Lancashire charity which helps local people recover and rebuild their lives after suffering heart illness.

She was passionate about working and fundraising as it fulfilled in her the desire to meet people, to pass on encouragement and her love of life in general.
.
Through Heidi, Sophie and Naomi this passion to meet and encourage others continued through school life and the twin group she set up in Preston

Throughout her journey in life, Laura never faltered in her passion to encourage others, either through example, through her writings or her faith.

For God did not give us a spirit of timidity, but a spirit of power of love and of self-discipline. So do not be ashamed to testify about our Lord.

From Tara Stephenson - Sister-in-law

Like a powerful staff in your hands;
Courage, truth and strength you showed,
Crazy faith, always wrapped around you like a glorious royal robe,
In perfect obedience, you always knew just what your purpose was,
And when those around you doubted, you'd wink,
Give one of your massive smiles and simply say,
"But you don't know my God!"

One amazing Hero, Three beautiful Princesses, adventures aplenty:
Oh how 'Team Stevo' made your heart burst,
Dancing, singing, funny, selfless; cheeky
Lol, your family always came first,
And in the midst of it all, no matter how tough it got,
We all looked on in wonder as you'd still declare,
"How great is my God!"

Oh Lol, I wish I could have heard the triumphant welcome
From Heaven's Angel armies,
And as He placed that crown on your head,
I wish I could have seen those glorious stars and dazzling rubies,
I wish the throne room had a secret earthly window,
More than anything else in this world,
So I could have seen Jesus gently whisper to His Father,
"Lord, how amazing is our girl!"

Tributes read by Alan Lewis – Laura's High School Head Teacher

"You have lived with fierce determination and have shown such grit; you have taught us how to live. I mean, how to really LIVE - to live like you. To revel in every moment. To walk with grace, positivity and passion. To have faith and hope in the face of adversity. To love unconditionally and prioritise the needs of those around us, even when facing our own struggles - however mountainous. "

"We have been blessed beyond measure to have known you, to have loved you, to have shared so many life-changing occasions and moments together. Our world is forever changed. In honour of you, we count our blessings. We thank God for your life, and we thank you for the many ways in which you have enhanced and blessed the lives of all of us, the privileged many who have been lucky enough to know you."

"It can't be said enough how amazing Laura was & how inspiring,"

"Harriet, silently I have followed you and your sister for years. You were blessed to have a sister like her."

"I feel so lucky I got to meet her and spend time getting to know her. My mum also had chemo last year which generally was the same time Laura was having hers so we always popped in for a chat and chatted anything other than chemo. Everyone loved her so much'"

"I loved our chats and I always left feeling so uplifted and inspired. She really is such a special person."

"She was always a fighter! Everyone from uni. is in tears over the news but that just shows how many people she touched."

"You will **always** be 3 sisters!!Nothing can ever change that. Laura was always so positive and really was a warrior."

"She was so amazing to me, especially in the last year, despite everything she was going through."

"She was a truly brave and inspirational woman. You must have been so proud by how she lived so passionately. It was a pleasure to have known her so long."

"Laura was one of the many highlights of my uni years and was loved by everyone."

"I was so inspired by Laura and her strength and spirit. I can see just from the photos Heidi, Sophie and Naomi have definitely got the same."

"Laura's earthly life may have been too short, but the footprint she has left is lasting and significant through her inspirational faith and loving family."

"I have fond memories of Laura from when we were growing up and her courage and strength is truly an inspiration to us all."

"Laura is such an Inspiration and hero! She fought with everything."

"Your radiant girl is radiant still and continuing to fully express Life and Love with her irrepressible joy and certain knowledge that she is embraced in the arms of everlasting Love."

"Laura was so vibrant and is so vivid in my mind,"

"Laura was such a lovely person with a beautiful smile and fire of determination in her eyes and I will remember her with much love and deep respect."

"Warrior girl is such a wonderful description of a beautiful girl that has navigated this journey with courage and a heart for others. Laura has touched each of our lives for good & we will each treasure our own memories."

"Laura's indomitable spirit will be an inspiration to all."

"Growing up with Laura was truly a blessing, a real inspiration; a true light in my life."

"As a pupil Laura was exemplary – "the best head girl the school never had" was our standing joke. Laura was a remarkable, talented and determined young lady who left her mark in life and will be sorely missed."

"It was a privilege to know her and watch her develop into a beautiful person."

"Even as a child she had a fun and caring spirit that shone through."

"Our minds keep going back to our wonderful times in France Laura was such a lovely girl."

"Laura was a beautiful person inside and out She had a wonderful faith which she wasn't afraid to share with people she met."

"Never did she shine so brightly as in her illness and even through the dark times she will always be an inspiration."

"She came into our lives and has changed us forever and made us all better people. She was the blessing that God sent us. Truly blessed to have met her."

"Laura will remain in our hearts forever."

Mike Barnes – Dad

On 4th September 1983 at about 8.00 a.m. I found myself driving home from the Cambridge maternity hospital, walking into a church, just standing in the church which I had never walked into before, wanting to tell someone about the miracle that had just happened in our lives. A cleaner came up and asked could she help. Tears came into my eyes, I was incapable of speech and I just walked out. Some 36 years later I'm back in a church, which I have never been in before, tears in my eyes but this time I'm going to tell you, well try anyway, why I'm here.

What was it like to have Laura as a daughter? Remembering the times throughout her life, when she was unsure what to do, she would ask "Dad, what should I do? School, University, boyfriends, jobs, and I'd try to answer her best I could; just as Dads do. And then 13 days ago she asked me the same question "My body's had enough Dad tell me what to do" And this time I had no answer

It was my original thought to go through lots of stories both funny and sad about the person we all knew initially as Laura Barnes and later Laura Stephenson ...., but actually the best person to really, really tell you about Laura is Laura herself So I went back to her first few blogs And make no apologies for reading parts of them and you get a far better insight into the Laura that she had developed into ......

From Laura's blog .... *"I am placed in the PERFECT position now to help others HE knows what is needed for me to bless others while fighting this battle, so that's what I will do!*
Last week was a big deal for me as I got my wig, my hair isn't gone but has thinned dramatically. After being told mixed messages over whether I would lose my hair or not I wasn't quite sure how I felt about it. I had two mini tears moments with Mark but other than that figure it looks ok & it isn't forever so let's get cracking!

After purchasing the chosen locks, I was in work the next day when I got a phone call from an upset daughter of a lady who had been diagnosed with breast cancer. Mother and daughter were panicking about losing hair and wearing a wig. It was great to say "I did that

146

yesterday, it's not too bad". All of these are my opinions but I do believe that in this position. GOD has great plans for people for me to bless and conversations that have impact.

Not a path I would have ever chosen but man am I excited to see what HE has in store not only for those I come into contact with but ultimately for me! "

There aren't many times I let the side effects get to me but last night I can honestly say I was exhausted so at 8pm, bedtime beckoned and I took it! I must admit I don't have a massive problem with chemo, it's a necessity and it's making this thing go so I figure may as well just get on with it. I also get a good three hours a week of quiet reading time so who can complain at that with three children who keep you on the go I think what makes my chemo sessions even more interesting is the people I am meeting. The last few times I have met someone just embarking on this journey and looking terrified. I'm not sure I was as terrified but I think the fear of not knowing what you will feel like at the end of the cycle often adds to this fear. We chatted and at the end of the session we both had smiles on our faces. I have loved chatting to people and hopefully helping to put their mind at ease. There really is nothing to fear of chemo. You manage the side effects and aim to not let them take on a mind of their own by bringing you down in your spirit. I don't really think too much of what these horrible chemicals are doing to my body as they may be nasty but they need to be to destroy that bigger mountain of tumours.

People keep telling me that I am so positive about things and I am never quite sure how to respond... I can say that I don't feel like that every day and some days I have to work hard at it. The thing is with being positive; it is a choice. We have the freedom to choose how we approach something. Now don't get me wrong I have days just like everyone else where our stresses and problems seem like this huge weight on your shoulders and we just can't shift it, and so it affects our mood too. But being given the freedom to choose how we face those things in front of us, is something that I wouldn't swop for anything. It allows me to FIGHT and to make sure that each day, regardless of how I feel, I am standing steadfast in the promises that are given to me. How amazing that I get to choose how I want to deal with something!

147

And every time I choose FAITH over fear, HOPE over worry and BELIEF over doubt. It's not always easy but it is definitely worth it.

For most of us with cancer all we want is someone to fight with us and tell us that's what they are doing
This is my promise; I stand on it because I know the power of my God • to all those people who stand beside me thank you • to all those who look at me & say 'you look so well' thank you • to those that fight &; pray with me thank you • you are my constant source of positivity and I love you for it! •

and I would like, on behalf of Mark, Heidi, Sophie, Naomi and all of our family, those doctors that said 'Would you like us to throw everything we have at this?' ----; to those District nurses who put Laura as their number 1 person and were on hand 24 hours a day always with a huge smile and reassurance ;   to Heartbeat who gave her hope to carry on working –, to all those who sent her messages of hope and love; to the parents in the playground who gave her amazing words of support; to all of you here today; Thank you for your hope and positivity;   Interestingly Laura went onto say……..

"for those that tilt their head to one side, give me that 'I'm sorry' look; please don't be because you don't have any idea of the power of the God I serve

it's never easy to know what to say (I understand that) but equally we all have one thing in common ………… the desire to Fight."

Since all this started people keep saying I need to write things down. My story. I'm not sure much of what I have to say will be interesting to all but I do know that I am seeing little God instances all the time. So before I start with those let me also say that I will unashamedly be talking about my walk with God throughout this journey because without Him it would be a battle without hope and I can tell you now that would be one scary path

I, however, don't have to experience that because just like my own Dad on Earth, I have a Father in heaven that would also move mountains for me. With God NOTHING is IMPOSSIBLE!"

148

So maybe, just maybe 13 days ago Laura wasn't talking to me, Change the word Dad for Father ...... "Father, tell me what to do" and maybe he answered far better than I.

So you see I didn't know her as well as she knew herself. Her words are far more powerful than any I could write   And its only now in the last few days that the person that I used to say ... "aw well that's Laura" was in fact an amazing person that I took for granted. A person that inspired others; a person that was hugely regarded by others; a person that was loved by and loved, so many people. So actually I'm probably not the best person to talk about Laura. She is.......

Just close your eyes. ...   Picture her,....   And ask your question......

She **will** answer .

What next ?

Laura would have loved the fact
that so many people were reading her words.

Thank you on behalf of all her family and friends

If you have enjoyed reading this book as much as I've enjoyed putting
it together, please write a review. Do this via your online retailer

Alternatively do this by commenting
via Laura's blog on

www.warriordiaries.co.uk

Lightning Source UK Ltd.
Milton Keynes UK
UKHW040631290422
402257UK00001B/71